FROM A TOAD

THE JOURNEY TO THE KINGDOM

by Darrell W. Faucett

Cover by Claudia Gadotti

All biblical quotes taken directly from the King James Version

of the Bible

To my wonderful wife, Dorothea Grace, without your support and encouragement, this book would not be possible.

I also want to thank my mother, Charlene Heatley, for taking me to church as a youth. Those planted seeds have grown into the man I am today.

"To God be the glory, great things He has done"

Contents

Page

Introduction

From a Toad to a Prince, the Journey to the Kingdom is a fantasy version of true-to-life events in the life of our main character. From the time of his youth, Lerrad was easily influenced. This became a problem as he was coerced into going places and doing things unhealthy for him. As we follow the story, we find that nothing could impart happiness until he was invited on a journey that changed everything. I invite you to read this book with an open mind and an expectant heart. We all know someone, if not ourself, who has been struggling through life, wandering around like a cork in the water, tossed about with things beyond our control. The forces around us seem to make it impossible to accomplish what we want to in life. In this little story, things and people in his life influence Lerrad beyond his control. Addictions, among most, are something that transpires and usually without anyone even noticing what happened. It starts so innocently, and then morphs into a monster we cannot fight on our own. The author hopes you may see a small part of yourself in Lerrad and see that change is possible. Are you ready to embark on a trek you will never forget? Are you prepared for your journey to the kingdom?

Let us begin.

THE BEGINNING

Once upon a time, in a land not so far away, lived a toad name Lerrad. His home was on the far side of a vast country, next to a small pond where he was born. Lerrad had grown up like any other toads, and as a tadpole, his life was carefree, and he could swim around the pond with his two brothers and one sister whenever he wanted. The pond was a deep blue surrounded by many trees and beautiful red and yellow tulips. There were also fantastic-looking bright yellow daffodils with a sweet smell of perfume. On this warm spring day, it was also a highly active day for Lerrad. The aromas wafting through the air were a mixture of sweet florals with the hint of fresh pine boughs. Lerrad grew and spent more and more time on the banks of this beautiful blue pond. He would notice the smells more and more as the spring moved into longer days with warmer weather.

The day that Lerrad became fully developed, he had lost his tail, yet he could swim around the pond with outstanding precisions, back and forth. He would swim and often play games with his brothers and sister. Spring was such a wonderful time for Lerrad as he developed more and more into an adult toad, yet he was still a juvenile in his developmental process. What joy he experienced each day while swimming and playing around with friends he had met at the pond. A couple of his new friends suggested they explore the forest around the pond. Being prone to excitement, Lerrad agreed, and off they went. The woods were a little scary at first for Lerrad, filled was strange sounds and smells. The further they went, the more excited Lerrad became, and within a short time, they arrived at a clearing of beautiful green grass the likes of which Lerrad had never seen. On the opposite side of the clearing was a little water stream with a small waterfall as it entered the grassy area.

One boy exclaimed, "Look, some water, I don't know about you, but I'm thirsty." They all agreed and went to the waterfall to get a drink. Walking to the waterfall, Lerrad could not help looking around at all the beautiful plants and flowers. The colors were bright blue with purple hues within the plant, and the grass was bright green. There was an abundance of different bugs around the flowers, which distracted Lerrad as he was becoming hungry. "Over here," exclaimed Sam, one of the boys who were with the group. Lerrad turned from the flowers and ran to the waterfall where his friends were already drinking the water. "This water tastes different," mentioned one of the groups. When Lerrad dipped his tongue into the water, he said, "tastes warm and bitter." They all decided it was still okay to drink, and they did just that. Remembering his stomach was still empty, Lerrad led the way back to where he had seen the flowers and bugs. Before he could reach the area, he turned to the friend and said, "I feel a little woozy." Sam told him, "we just need to eat."

Arriving at the flowers, they all ate their fill of delicious bugs surrounding the air of the blue and purple flowers. "I feel much better," Lerrad stated, then added, "I need some more of that water." Off they went to the other side of the clearing to the waterfall. They all drank until it satisfied them. Realizing they were all feeling different, Lerrad exclaimed, "Wow, I feel good," and talked about anything and everything that came to his mind. He talked about his brothers and how they played hide-and-seek the day he lost his tail. On and on, he talked. None of them noticed, and others joined them. All were going to the waterfall for a drink as well.

Suddenly several toads were hopping around, drinking, eating, and talking to each other. Lerrad could not help noticing that many of the crowd ate some leaves from the purple flower plants and could not resist. He wanted to taste some of this for himself. "These are good," he said, and added, "sweet and sticky though." As Lerrad went back and forth for another taste of the sweet sticky plant, someone that had come to the clearing said, "Not so much, that's all there is right now, and the plants need to grow more leaves for the next time." Lerrad agreed and headed back to the waterfall for another drink and realized he felt different, bold and happy like nothing he had ever known. Back at the waterfall, he met a girl name Neera and talked with her.

"Have you been here before?" she asked.

"Yes, and there's another waterfall to the northside of here. I would like to see that someday," replied Lerrad.

On and on, they chatted until the sunset beyond the forest.

"I should go home," stated Lerrad.

"Don't you want to kiss me?" asked Neera.

"I have never kissed before," replied Lerrad.

"I will show you how," said Neera.

Giggling as their lips pursed together, Lerrad felt warm all over. After the kiss, Lerrad stated he needed to go home before his mother worried.

"Can I meet you again?" said Neera.

"I would like that," replied Lerrad.

They agreed between the two of them, and they would meet at the same spot at the end of the week. Lerrad hopped toward his home and was feeling wheezy and tired and was glad he was almost home when he entered his house, which was a hollowed-out stump where his family lived.

His mother exclaimed, "Where have you been, I was worrying?"

To change the subject, Lerrad asked, "What's for dinner? I'm starving."

His mother replied, "We have roasted beetles with fern salad and dried ants for dessert, but you still need to answer my question. Where have you been? Your brothers said that they hadn't seen you since lunch."

Lerrad answered his mother, "My new friends and I went for a walk through the forest and found beautiful green grass with purple flowers and some funny-tasting water."

"What!" his mother screamed, "you went to mara?"

Puzzled, Lerrad could not understand why his mother was so mad. She continued, "Please tell me you didn't drink the water."

Looking down Laird replied "yes."

"That water is no good. It causes you to do strange things. That is why your father no longer lives with us."

Lerrad had given no thought to why his father had left, assuming it was just something all toads do when they are older. "I'm sorry, mom," said Lerrad.

"Just promise me, you will stay away from the mara, go clean up and come to dinner," Lerrad's mom said.

After eating his dinner, Lerrad went to bed, yet he could not sleep, as his mind would not be quiet from the discussion with his mother to the wonderful time he had at the green field and how he had kissed a girl for the first time. Remembering he told Neera he would meet her at the end of the week.

"What was wrong with the mara?" he thought to himself. It had made him feel better than he had ever felt in his life. His mother would be furious at him, yet he knew he had to go back to meet Neera. Finally, Lerrad fell asleep. The next day Lerrad realized after waking up, he did not feel so good. His head was hurting, and he was very thirsty. After getting some water and eating breakfast, he felt a little better, yet the entire day he was not himself. The week went by slowly for Lerrad, and his mind was continually on Neera and how she made him feel. He had never had such a feeling and wanted to be with her all the time.

NEERA

Finally, the day had arrived. He was going to sneak off to meet Neera at the grassy clearing. He had planned out exactly how he would leave the pond and head to his heart's desire. He waited until his mother was inside to start dinner, and then he made his move. Off he ran to the woods as fast as he could go. As he entered deeper into the forest, he suddenly realized he was alone, unlike the first time. The sounds and smells frightened him, coercing him to run faster, yet he became out of breath and had to stop to rest. Even though Lerrad was focused on meeting up with Neera, he could not help but wonder what his mother would think when she found him gone. Once Lerrad had collected himself, he continued on his way. He felt the time was going slow in his heart, yet before he realized it, he had made it to the clearing where he had met Neera just days before.

After he realized where he was, Lerrad began looking around to see if Neera was there yet waiting for him. She had not arrived, yet a few others were roaming around the clearing.

Lerrad decided he should get a drink after all the running he had done. Once at the waterfall, he thought about his mother's words. She had said the mara was bad. He thought to himself, "it cannot be that bad, I drank it last time, and nothing bad happened." Not remembering how he felt the day after, Lerrad dipped himself into the mara to get a drink, hearing a familiar voice calling, "Lerrad." He at once realized it was Neera. His heart fluttered as he turned to see her face. "Over here," she called as Lerrad moved to meet her at the spot she was standing.

"Have you been here long?" Neera asked?

"No, I just got here," replied Lerrad.

"Good, let's go get a drink," said Neera, and off they went to the waterfall.

Lerrad noticed the water was not as bitter as he remembered, yet it was still warm inside his belly. After drinking their fill, Lerrad and Neera talked about their time apart and how they could not stop thinking about each other.

The two noticed the clearing was filling with others who came to drink this magic water, and all were lining up for a drink.

"Let's go to the other side and get something to eat," suggested Lerrad.

"Okay," replied Neera, and off they went.

Once at the place of the purple plant, where the bugs did gather, Lerrad noticed that most of the plants had thinned out, looking skinny and weak.

"We better eat some of these plants before they're gone," said Neera, and Lerrad agreed.

The two of them went to eat the bugs and the purple plants. They had both received their fill, yet Neera said, "We should eat a little more of the plants; once they're gone, they won't be back until next year."

Lerrad took the hint and continued to eat the purple plant until he could not eat any more. Before he knew what was happening, Lerrad felt like he had never felt before, his ears were ringing, and his stomach was rocking back and forth.

He was seeing things moving around his head, then realized they were not there at all.

"I feel funny," said Lerrad.

"That will go away soon, and you'll feel happy all over. Let's get some more of the water, and we will be just fine," said Neera.

True to her words, by the time they had reached the line at the waterfall, Lerrad felt giggly and was laughing for no reason at all. While waiting their turn to get a drink, it was obvious, the field of grass was full of other toads. They were all milling about, talking, and drinking. Someone yelled "PARTY!" out of nowhere.

"What is that?" Lerrad asked.

"It means let's all have fun, drink, and eat until we're having a good time," replied Neera.

"Okay," said Lerrad.

When their turn to drink came, Lerrad guzzled as much as he could hold inside his stomach. He came out yelling "PARTY," which set off an echo of the word *party* throughout the group. It was apparent the clearing was so full, they were all bumping into each other, to the point of crowding.

"Over here," shouted Neera.

Lerrad had not even noticed he was separated from Neera until she had called out. When he got to where Neera was standing, she said, "Let's go for a walk."

So Lerrad followed Neera into the woods to get away from the crowd. Walking only a short distance, they came upon a partially hollowed log and crawled inside.

"Do you like me?" Neera asked.

"Oh yes," said Lerrad, I thought about you the whole time we were apart."

Neera replied, "Do you want to kiss me"?

To that Lerrad said, "Yes, I do," and Neera plunged to the awaiting lips of Lerrad.

It was several hours, they kissed and talked about their feelings for each other. It was easy to snuggle with Neera, Lerrad thought, and they kissed, touched, and talked for hours, continuing until the early hours of the next day when they fell asleep in each other's arms. Lerrad's sleep was shallow and consumed with many thoughts he could not turn off. When Lerrad finally fell into a deep sleep, he had a dream that confused and frightened him very much.

The vision he saw was of a man dressed in a white robe, sitting on a white horse. The man said, "Follow me!" then rode away. This vision woke Lerrad up, leaving him trembling in fear. (Remember, Lerrad was a toad and had never seen either a man or a horse.) Lerrad felt the gentle, comforting touch of Neera and settled down to fall back to sleep. Neera was the first to arise when the sun had come up and gently caressed Lerrad until he awoke. "Good morning," she said, and Lerrad returned with "Good morning."

Immediately, Lerrad realized he felt awful. His head was spinning, and his stomach was very sick.

"You need to drink some water and get something to eat," Neera said.

"Not the mara," Lerrad said, I think that's what made me sick."

Neera replied, "You're right. It takes time to get used to the mara water. Come, I will show you some pure water."

Lerrad agreed and followed Neera to a freshwater stream, where he plunged himself into the water and drank until he could not drink any more. When he came out of the water, Neera had set out some tender bugs and fresh maple leaves for him to eat. "Thank you," Lerrad said and ate the food Neera had brought him. Lerrad still felt sick, but not as bad as it was when he first woke up. Remembering his mother's words about the mara, he asked, "What is this mara water?"

"It comes from a stream that goes to the south and comes from a place far away to the north. Some say it's bad, and others like it a lot." Neera continued, "the further north you go, the stronger it is, and the further south it becomes weaker."

Lerrad was having a hard time understanding and asked, "Why does it make you feel so good after drinking it and so bad the next day?"

Neera answered, "Most have different opinions, yet we all know that the more you drink it, the easier it gets each time.

Also, we mixed it with the purple flowers. They have a feeling all on their own, but when you mix them, it intensifies the mara."

Lerrad was still trying to deal with this and the newness of a girl in his life, and suddenly he remembered the dream. It was just a nightmare, he reasoned, brought on by the mara, yet he could not get the picture out of his head. What was it that he saw, and what did it mean "follow me?" As the day went on, Lerrad did feel better and was able to concentrate on his new relationship with Neera. With that, he was also thinking about his mom. "I bet she is distraught," Lerrad thought, but to him, nothing was more important than Neera.

THE FAMILY

Several days went by, and as the seasons started to change into fall, Neera and Lerrad were inseparable. It had also been some time since Lerrad had seen his mother, and he decided Neera and he would go to visit his mom. The two lovers agreed and set off to Lerrad's childhood home. It was not far from where the two had been staying, only a short distance from the grassy clearing and the mara. Lerrad entered the house first and received an emotional greeting from his mother. She sobbed for joy at seeing her son. She did not know what had happened to him. Lerrad then called for Neera and introduced her as his mate. This thrilled his mother, and she immediately embraced Neera. They all talked for hours and caught up with each other. After a good night's sleep, Lerrad took Neera to the pond where he grew up, and they both went for a swim. Neera announced this would be the perfect place to start a family, on the far side of the pond. She decided to lay a group of eggs next to the shore for Lerrad to become a father. The two of them kissed for some time and, as the sun was going down, became excited to tell Lerrad's mother.

When they came back into the house, Lerrad announced they would have tadpoles of their own and build their home across the pond. This news thrilled Lerrad's mom, and she volunteered to help with the children after they hatched. The following day Lerrad went to see his mother alone because he had many questions for her.

"Tell me about my father," Lerrad asked.

"He was a good father and always took care of us," she answered.

"You said he left because of the mara," continued Lerrad.

"He began to spend more and more time at places with mara, then found someone else. He then decided to go off with her," answered Lerrad's mom. "I know you have been drinking the mara yourself, and I just ask you be careful not to let it take over your life."

Lerrad replied, "I won't."

He then asked his mom about the dream he had, and if she knew what "follow me" meant. She began to explain, "You left before I could tell you of things to expect in this world. There are many things you need to know."

Lerrad exclaimed, "Tell me, I want to know."

His mother began, "There are many things that will try to destroy you, always be on guard. Many of the elders tell a story about good and evil forces, and your worst enemy are the serpents. They hide and wait for you to come near them and attack before you know they are there. Always be careful and keep your eyes open at all times. As for the dream," Lerrad's mom continues, "there are stories of a king far to the east that sent his son to rescue all who will follow him to the kingdom, but I have never heard of anyone seeing him in person."

Lerrad asked, "I did see Him in my dream, but how can I follow Him if no one has seen him?"

His mom confirmed, "I don't know, son, but you should always follow your heart and watch out for the serpents."

This was a lot for Lerrad to absorb, and he realized the days of his carefree life had ended and that he was beginning the start of a new chapter in his life.

RESTLESS TIMES

Indeed a new chapter in the life of our beloved Lerrad had begun. As the children grew, it was the job of Lerrad to search and bring home food for his entire family, including his mother. At first, life seemed right, and everyone was happy and healthy—all except Lerrad. After collecting food, he had begun sneaking off to the mara for a drink from time to time. This arrangement did not seem to be a problem in the beginning, yet the days turned into weeks, and the weeks turned into months.

It was clear Lerrad was spending a considerable amount of time at the mara. Each time Lerrad went, he drank more and more, and eventually it began to cause problems at home. Part of the problem was that Neera was occupied with the children and was jealous of Lerrad because she also enjoyed the mara. Eventually, Neera began asking Lerrad's mother to watch the children so that she could join Lerrad at the waterfall of mara. The two would go off to drink and, frequently, came home late in the evening, intoxicated. Once winter sat in, the cold and snowy days made it impossible for them to go to what was turning out to be their favorite place to be. Lerrad's mother warned the two of them and asked them to spend less of their time drinking. Because of the weather, they agreed to stay home and spend more time with the children.

Throughout the winter, Lerrad, having a more focused thought, began to think more on the vision he had of the man on the white horse. He replayed the scene over and over in his mind. Unfortunately, the fright from the image confused him, and he decided this was why he had such a desire to drink, declaring that when he was drinking, the encounter of that frightful dream was distorted and put upon a shelf. One day it was all he could stand, and he knew he had to sneak off to visit the mara. When the time was right, he made his move, and out the door he went. The snow had stopped, yet there was much of it about the ground and on the trees. The air was crisp, and the beauty of the snow-covered landscape was astonishing, and Lerrad could not help but notice the wonders of this snow-flocked view.

The further he went, the more he realized how bitter cold it had become. This seasonal weather, Lerrad concluded, was why most toads remained in hibernation during the winter. Lerrad had come to his senses and realized he needed to find shelter. It was good for him that he was in the deepest part of the forest, which he had navigated many times, and knew of a fallen log that he could hide under to rest a while from the cold. Because of the cold, his reasoning was dulled, and he had not noticed how close he was to the stream of mara. Before long, he dozed off to a sound sleep beneath the log. It was not long before the man on the white horse once again visited Lerrad. Because he had rehearsed this vision in his head so many times, there were questions he wanted to ask.

"Who are you?" asked Lerrad.

"I am the Word, the Son of the great and mighty King," said the man.

Emboldened further, Lerrad asked," Before, you said to follow you, how will I know the way?" asked Lerrad. "*I am the way, the truth, and the life; when you seek me, you will find me when you search for me with all of your heart*," and just like that, the man rode away on his horse as he had come.

Lerrad had spent the whole night sleeping under the log, and when morning came, he had a strange desire inside himself. He wanted to find out about the man on the white horse, realizing where he was and where he was going the night before. He determined to go home and forget about the mara for the time being.

Lerrad headed home, tracking through the snow until he arrived at his destination. Inside the house he was met by an angry Neera.

"Don't you love me?" asked Neera.

"Yes, I do," said Lerrad.

The two talked for some time, and Lerrad had the chance to explain his dream or vision to her, letting her know he needed to go on a trek to find the meaning of this thing. Lerrad also went over to his mom to see if she knew anything more about this man in the white robe. She explained to Lerrad the only thing she could suggest is that Lerrad go to the pond's elder, where he might find the answer.

Lerrad took his mother's advice and went to the elder of the pond asking, "Do you know of the man in a white robe on a white horse?"

He said, "follow me, but I don't know where to go."

The elder began to tell Lerrad the story of a king who lived in the far northeast who sent his son whose name is Jesus, into the uttermost part of his kingdom to bring his chosen back to the king.

"What must I do to find this son and the king?" Lerrad asked.

"You must search for him within yourself," continued the elder.

"Ancient words say, you must believe in the king and his son and be born again." replied the elder.

"What means this, born again? How can it be?" asked Lerrad.

"Your quest will begin when you decide this is what you desire with all of your heart, then you will find who you are inside. Find yourself and commit to this journey with your whole heart, and then you will find your way," replied the elder.

This information was a lot for Lerrad to take in, yet he was committed in his heart that he wanted to take the journey to find the king's son that he may follow him to the kingdom.

Lerrad did try to find the answers within himself, and at first, he was dedicated to following his heart to finding the path to the kingdom. Several weeks went by, and the weeks turned into years, and during this time, Lerrad did not have any other visions of the man on the white horse.

Eventually, Lerrad became less committed to the quest and returned to the mara and purple plants. In fact, that was all he thought about, the mara. Lerrad excused his habit, believing he was led back to the bitter water because of Neera. She had also taken a greater interest in spending time at the spring of mara. After a few more years, Lerrad started building a tolerance to mara's original potency, and the purple plants became less and less available.

Because of many disagreements between Lerrad and Neera, Lerrad decided he had to leave Neera and the children to find the stream of stronger water. He had thought about going for some time. It was now he reasoned and left. It was late spring, and Lerrad had known the stronger mara was to the north of the original waterfall, so he followed the stream north. The farther he went, he would taste the mara to see how strong it had become. Lerrad realized it had not changed much, if any, and he realized that it would be a long journey.

NITA

Lerrad found a nice clearing as the sun was setting and decided to drink his fill of mara then find a cozy spot to rest for the evening. Finding an area of tall grass and other plants, he snuggled in and fell to sleep relatively quickly. Upon awakening, Lerrad felt the all-to-familiar headache and queasy stomach with the need to find pure water and something to eat. Because he still needed to follow the mara stream, he did not go too far away from his original track. It took some time, but Lerrad did find a small pool of clear water and tasted it to see if it was good to drink. It was okay, and he drank until he started to feel better.

Looking around the pool, he noticed there were several different kinds of plants that he had never seen before. While tasting some of the plants, he noticed there was another toad also eating the plants. "Hello," Lerrad called out.

"Hello to you, my name is Nita. Have you been here before?" she asked.

"No, I am following the stream of mara to the stronger drink," replied Lerrad.

"Oh, that sounds like fun. Can I come with you?" Nita asks.

"Sure, it will be nice to have some company on the trip," said Lerrad.

Looking around at the different plants the two were tasting, Lerrad noticed a happy feeling after eating one of them. The plants were short with brownish seed-looking pods and beautiful red flowers. Lerrad asked Nita if she knew about the plants in this area. He knew the effects were different, yet more pleasant, than the purple plants from where he had come from. Nita replied that she was also passing through and knew little about the plants. After the two travelers ate and drank until they felt better, Lerrad announced they should be on their way. But first, he pulled down a few of the plants with pods to take on the journey, as he really enjoyed how they made him feel, and off they went, following the stream of mara to the north.

It was a warm and beautiful day, and the journey was filled with many new sights and wonders as this was an area where Lerrad had never been. The trees and plants that lined the stream were spectacular, with many different colors and hues of bright to lighter greens surrounded by flowers of every color, sending out an overwhelming scent of florals that amazed Lerrad. The pair found a widening area and decided to stop and rest because it was getting late in the day. This also gave them a chance to taste some of the mara to see if it was indeed getting more potent than it was downstream. Lerrad approached first and began to drink. Immediately he noted that it was more powerful, and that only after a few sips, he started feeling the effects of this magic water he had grown so fond of.

Nita followed after to get a drink, and the two of them continued until they had both become noticeably intoxicated. This brought about a conversation that lasted for hours. They talked about anything and everything that came to mind. After the sun went down, the pair found a cozy spot of tall grass to lay in for the night. They continued to talk, and before long, they were kissing and snuggling the entire evening, and soon, the sun began to rise. Lerrad and Nita were sure that they were having feelings for each other and determined to stay together as a couple.

They decided to set off to look for fresh water and something to eat as they both felt the effects of the mara, and the lack of sleep did amplify the need for clean water. It was only a short time before they found a small pond of clean water. Jumping in, they both drank their fill and swam around for some time before coming out for something to eat. They found some grubs and a couple of beetles that make them feel much better, yet Lerrad remembered the flower pods from the place where he had met Nita. He took one and gave one to Nita. Lerrad had realized he liked the way the pods had made him feel, so he hid some for himself for later. These flower pods also made them feel a little tired, so the two of them lay down and took a nap for several hours.

After waking up, Lerrad realized the flower pods had a way of totally relaxing him, and he loved the way they made him feel. He retrieved one of the pods he had saved, and ate part of it to make himself feel better. He had done this without Nita knowing. Once the couple had fully woken from the nap, Nita suggested they revisit the mara, and again the two spent many hours drinking and giggling and kissing. The pair had spent two days at this spot, and when the sun came up the second day, they both agreed it was time to continue their journey. After several days of traveling north, Lerrad and Nita noticed they were approaching an area with a higher population. Before long, they were at a place where the mara had collected into a large pond and was surrounded by many other toads. Lerrad also noticed that at the far north end of this pond was a sizable box-looking thing with smoke coming from the top and that out of the box at the lower end was a strange pipe with the mara dripping into the pond. Because of his distraction, Lerrad became separated from Nita and, at first, did not notice. Lerrad knew he had to taste the mara and see if it had changed.

Realizing this was the end of the journey, the mara's source was the pipe coming from the big box made out of trees. Sure enough, when Lerrad tasted the mara, it was the strongest of all he had tasted. Many toads were moving around and drinking this stronger mara. Conversations were loud surrounding the pond, and it was plain to see that all the toads were very intoxicated and rambling on and on with each other.

After drinking and talking with some in the group, Lerrad realized he had become separated from Nita. He started to look for her, and it did not take long before he saw her on the far bank drinking and laughing around with a couple of male toads. Just as he reached the spot where she was, Lerrad saw one of the other males go over and kiss Nita. She did not even notice Lerrad was standing there.

This, decided Lerrad, was time for him to also search for a different mate. There was such a large group of toads that it did not take Lerrad long to find a female toad for him to snuggle and kiss.

As the evening turned into the early morning, Lerrad had drunk so much of the mara, so he passed out on the bank's outer edge around the pond. When he woke up, the sun had risen, and he realized the girl he had met the day before was gone. Lerrad felt the mara's effects and was very sick to his stomach, and knew he needed some clean water soon. Looking around, it was apparent he would have to search for water as none was close. He was so desperate for a drink that he took a few sips of the mara. This decision did help a little, giving him enough strength to go looking for fresh water. It did not take long for Lerrad to notice a group of toads heading into the wooded area on the pond's east side and decided to follow them.

"Is there water over here?" Lerrad asked one of the groups.

"Yes," the toad replied.

"We are going to breakfast if you want to come."

Lerrad said, "Yes, I do. I feel pretty bad and need something to drink."

The group Lerrad was following arrived at a clearing surrounded by a stream of water and groups of other toads setting down with female toads, bringing them food and water to drink.

"What is this?" Lerrad asked.

"It's our eating spot," replied one of the toads.

"You sit down, and they bring your food and drink, and you pay them later by bringing food and water to the storehouse for the next meal."

Lerrad said, "Wow, that sounds great. I'm going to like it here."

After eating and rehydrating, Lerrad began to feel lonely for Nita and had hoped he would find her. But first, he needed to fill his obligation to the eating place to collect food for the next meal. One of the other toads showed Lerrad where to go and how to carry larger amounts of bugs and other food sources, ferns, leaves, and berries. Lerrad caught on fast and became very good at providing food for the eating place, thus securing his place to eat any time he wanted. Whenever he could, Lerrad would join others at the pond with the mara. The third day at the pond of mara, Lerrad spotted Nita on the far bank. He was so excited he hopped over to her as fast as he could go.

"I found you. I really missed you," he said. "I'm sorry," replied Nita. "I don't know what happens to me. If I drink too much, I can go for days and not remember where I was or what I did," she added.

"That's okay," said Lerrad, "that has happened to me before. I'm just glad I found you."

The two lovers spent every moment together possible. They decided between themselves that they would make their home in a place close to the mara. Nita and Lerrad spent a lot of time at the mara pond after Lerrad had finished work collecting food each day. On one of his days at work, Lerrad came across a familiar plant that he had once found on his mara journey. These were the short plants with the seed pods and red flowers. He had eaten all the ones from the trip and had not had any for several days. Lerrad decided he would pick as many of these plants as he could find and hide them in a particular spot in the woods he had seen once while looking for bugs. There he hid all he could find, then ate one, then took some back to his home. Lerrad and Nita lived in this place near the mara pond for over three years.

There Nita laid some eggs for Lerrad, yet only one egg hatched and became a girl toad. They named her Nileesha. The three lived in the same place for another two years, and in that time, Nita began drinking a smaller amount of the mara because of Nileesha. She also started having different health issues that lowered her interest in the mara. It seemed fine in the beginning, this did not deter Lerrad, and he continued drinking the mara and eating his flower pods, which caused him to become less dependable at his work. Eventually, Lerrad was told he could not eat at the eating place any longer. Lerrad determined he did not care and started finding ways to take care of himself and his family. However, this did not last long, and Lerrad was spending more time drinking and eating the pods and less and less time at home.

One day Nita and Lerrad were arguing over Lerrad's irresponsible behavior, and Nita told him to leave. Lerrad agreed it was time to go off on his own and left in search of a new place to live. After only a few days, Lerrad decided he would head back to his childhood home. He took all the flower pods he had hidden and headed down the mara's stream toward his childhood home.

THE DECISION

The journey home was slow and lonely for Lerrad, yet he decided he would be better off away from Nita. Within a few hours, Lerrad had reached the clearing where he had met Nita and decided he would rest there for the night.

After picking out a spot to sleep, he decided to drink his fill of the mara and eat some of the seed pods first. It did not take him long to realize he liked the feeling of the pods more than the mara, yet he continued to drink the mara and eat the pods until he passed out. Lerrad had never eaten that many of the pods before, and he was sent into a deep sleep.

Not long after Lerrad passed out, he was visited by a familiar figure, the man in the white robe on the white horse. This time the man called Lerrad by name. "Lerrad, why have you not followed me," said the man.

"I tried to follow but didn't know where you were," replied Lerrad.

"Because you didn't search with all of your heart, you have chosen instead to follow the serpent," said the man.

"I have seen no serpent," said Lerrad, yet remembered what his mother had said about watching out for the serpents. "I don't even know what the serpent is," replied Lerrad.

"The mara and the poppies you eat contain the serpent," continued the man on the white horse.

"But I don't understand," replied Lerrad.

"Before the sunrise, you will understand, and from tomorrow forward, you must search for the truth and follow me."

With that, the man on the white horse rode off from whence he came. This vision caused Lerrad to wake for just a short time, and then he was back to sleep. In fact, he fell into a deep sleep. Before long, an awful fear came to Lerrad, and he tossed and turned within his sleep. He then saw a beautiful woman wearing colorful clothing and adorned with sparkling

41

jewels of ear hangings, bracelets, and neck chains of shiny gold.

"Who are you?" asked Lerrad.

"Don't you recognize me, Lerrad?," asked the woman. "I have been your lover from the time of your youth. My name is Ethyl, the spirit within the drink you have chosen these many years. I have brought my sister, who you have also chosen to love."

From out of the shadows appeared a tall, slender figure clothed in a black robe with a hood covering the face. "Tell me you love me, Lerrad," said the figure in black.

"What is this you are saying? I don't even know you," said Lerrad.

"Of course you know me. I am the sister of Ethyl, my name is Ophelia, the spirit of death. I come from the flower pods you love so much!" The figure removed the hood, revealing a skull where a face should be and hair that appeared to move.

This terrified Lerrad, and he yelled out to the vision. "This is not true. You are only a dream of my sleep. Go away!" exclaimed Lerrad.

"You think you can dismiss us that easily?" the two spirits yelled together.

With that, the two converged into one being, a creature Lerrad had never seen, and they became a large snake with two heads. In a flash, they overtook Lerrad, wrapping coils around his small body.

When they had him securely wrapped the head of Ethyl said, "Tell me how much you love me, Lerrad."

"No," yelled Lerrad.

"That's right, tell her you love me more," said the head of Ophelia, and with this, Lerrad felt the coils tighten around him and could barely catch his breath. He felt like he was about to die.

In terror, Lerrad shouted, "Nooo! Please help me, Jesus, son of the king."

"Be quiet. You don't need him," said Ophelia.

This only strengthened Lerrad, and he yelled as loud as he could scream, "Help me please Jesus, son of the king. I will follow you the remainder of my life."

Instantly, the serpent of Ethyl and Ophelia turned Lerrad loose and disappeared. The whole experience had left Lerrad shaking in fear. When the morning sun broke over the horizon, Lerrad woke completely and noticed he felt better than he had in several years. There was no sick-feeling stomach or headache. He was, however, hungry and went to find something to eat.

He did not have far to go when he saw a lovely pond surrounded by a wide variety of bugs and fresh plants. Lerrad could not get over how he felt, as there was a joy inside him that was magnified beyond what he had known for a long time. Once Lerrad filled his belly, he decided to head on his way to his childhood home. He was conflicted in that part of him missed Nita and Nileesha, yet he knew the place he had come from was not good for him. Determined in his heart that he was done with the mara, and the pods, he continued on his way.

This trip was wonderful, and Lerrad noticed every detail of the trek. From the tall pine trees to the red and white clouds floating over his head, he smelled the smells of floral blossoms and heard the sounds of different birds singing among themselves. It was like he was in a whole new world, and he knew inside himself that a miracle had happened, and he had a grateful heart for what had happened within him. It did not take long before Lerrad recognized his home and became excited with joy.

The first thing to pop into his view was the little pond he had so much fun swimming in, and he could not resist jumping in for a quick dip. As he reached the far end of the pond, he saw his mother coming out of the house and called out to her, "Mom, I'm home." It took a minute for her to recognize Lerrad as he was coming out of the water until he again said, "it's me, Lerrad." This brought Lerrad's mom to tears as she had not seen him for some time. Lerrad crawled out of the pond and ran to her, giving her a huge hug and kiss.

"My son, I have missed you so much," said Lerrad's mom.

"I missed you too," Lerrad replied.

The two walked to the little house in the hollowed-out log where Lerrad spent the first years of his life. It was a grand reunion, and the two of them traded stories as Lerrad's mom started dinner for them. As their conversation continued, Lerrad filled his mom in on the breakup of him and Nita. When Lerrad asked about Neera, his mother was sad to tell Lerrad that Neera had passed away and that the children had gone away on their own. This obviously saddened Lerrad, and his mother quickly consoled him. After dinner, Lerrad and his mother continued to catch up with each other. At one point, Lerrad explained the vision he had just days before. Lerrad's mother realized this was something special and that Lerrad needed to search this king out at all cost. She then suggested Lerrad go back to the elder and follow the path to the king. The following day Lerrad did just that. He went to the elder to find out as much information as possible about this king and his son Jesus.

Lerrad recited all of his visions to the elder. "Where do I start?" he asked.

"There is a man, just a day's journey to the east, who is said to have direct communication with the king and his son," explained the elder.

With this new information, Lerrad went back to his mother and made arrangements for him to leave in the morning. Lerrad tossed and turned throughout the night as the excitement of his upcoming journey was all he could think of. Finally, Lerrad drifted off to sleep. He had not been asleep very long when he was visited by a familiar vision. It was the man in the white robe, except this time he was not on a horse.

He began to speak to Lerrad. "I know your heart and have called you to follow me to the kingdom of God," he said.

"Who is this God?" Lerrad asked.

"He is my father and desires that you become part of our family," the man answered.

"What must I do?" asked Lerrad.

"You must be born again," said Jesus.

"Go to the man named Mark who the elder spoke of, and there you will find the answers you seek."

This excited Lerrad so much he woke up early and was set to go. He and his mother said their goodbyes and embraced each other as Lerrad's mom handed him some food to take with him on his journey.

LERRAD'S CONVERSION

Lerrad could hardly contain himself. Inside of him was an overwhelming joy he had not ever felt, a peace that was stronger than anything he could explain. The view he experienced along the trip was magnified, and Lerrad noticed every detail of the trail, from the smells of different trees to the softness of the ground beneath his feet. The day was warm, the sky was blue, and the birds sang a melody like no other Lerrad had heard. In the midday heat, Lerrad came across a small stream surrounded on both sides with beautiful bright and colorful flowers of every kind. As Lerrad bent down to drink, he whispered the words to himself, "Please be clean water, not the mara." Sure enough, it was the freshest clean water he could remember drinking. He followed up his drink with a slight sigh of "thank you!"

After drinking the water and eating his lunch, it did not take Lerrad long to doze off under a shady tree. There he contemplated the many things he had gone through in his life, and how excited he was to be on this journey of a lifetime. After awaking, Lerrad set off in the direction of his destination, yet he seemed to be walking with a little dance to each step. Lerrad felt happier than he could remember. Before long, Lerrad reached his destination, it was a small clearing with a tiny pond fed by a stream of the clearest water Lerrad had ever seen. On the east side of the pond was a little house made out of smooth stones that were held together with mud from around the pond, with a window on the north side, and the door was made out of patches of different colored leaves from around the house.

Lerrad called out, "Hello, is Marc here?"

A faint voice replied, "Who's there?"

Lerrad replied, "My name is Lerrad, and I was sent by the elder of the pond to the west of here."

"What can I do for you?" the little voice replied.

"I search for the son of the king to the east." From the shadows appeared a small man with gray hair and a round face. "You are a man, not a toad," exclaimed Lerrad.

"You are a toad and not a man," replied the little man, with a slight chuckle. "Come inside and rest," continued the man.

Lerrad followed Marc inside the little house and was surprised at how large it was inside. The light from the window illuminated the entire room, and Lerrad was puzzled by the things he saw inside the house. On one side of the room was a table with four little chairs, and on the table was a bouquet of beautiful flowers. In the same area was a box and another table without chairs, and on that table were all different things that Lerrad concluded to be different food than he had ever seen. Continuing his gaze around the little house, in the other room was a longish log carved into a sitting bench surrounded with two larger chairs on the other side of the bench. Lerrad was so confused he had to ask the man what this was.

"Sit down over here," the man said as he pointed to a spot on the bench, as he took a seat on one of the two chairs at the end of the bench. "Why did you come to me?" Marc asked.

Lerrad began to tell him of all of the things he had been through, how he was visited several times by a man called Jesus in his dreams, and of the terrible vision of the spirits of Ethyl and Ophelia. Lerrad then asked Marc, "I was told you could help me find the way to the king and his son Jesus.

"Ahhh," replied Marc, "do you seriously want to know about the king, and are you ready to follow Him wherever He leads you?"

"Yes, oh yes, I do," exclaimed Lerrad.

"Alright then, let me call my wife to join us, and then we will start."

Mark got up and went through a small door into a different room. Lerrad could hear Marc talking to someone in the backroom. Shortly, the two emerged from the room.

"Hello, Lerrad," said the woman, "My name is Linda. Welcome to our home."

Linda was a lovely looking woman with the same gray hair as her husband, and her face glowed a bright radiance of light as if she were a star or the moon. Marc sat back on the little chair as Linda went to the table in the other room and fixed them something to eat.

It did not take Linda long to put together a meal for them to share, and she sat down to eat. Lerrad started to reach for something when Marc stopped him and said, "We like to thank God for every meal. Could you join us?" Lerrad did not know what that meant yet was polite and allowed Marc to continue. Marc then blessed the food and asked for guidance in all they do. After the blessing, Lerrad continued to eat his meal and noticed that he had never seen any of the food they were eating, yet every bite was wonderfully delicious. Once they were finished eating, Marc invited Lerrad to come back to the front area to sit and talk.

"Are you sure you are ready to search for and serve the king and his son, Jesus?"

With tears of Joy, Lerrad replied, "Oh yes, I am ready to give myself to the king and his son, Jesus."

Marc began to speak. "You must believe in your heart and in your mind first, that God is, and that he sent his son, Jesus, to forgive you and to change you into his perfect creation." Marc then continued, "Lerrad do you believe that God is, and that he sent his son?"

"Yes, I do," replied Lerrad.

"Do you also know that you are a sinner and ask God to forgive you of all the bad things you have done in your life?" asked Marc.

"Yes, I do, I am sorry for the bad I have done," continued Lerrad.

Marc then rehearsed words to make sure Lerrad understood that we are all sinners, that God loves us so much that he sent his only son to sacrifice his life for all who believe. How the son of God was hated by the leaders of that time, and they brutally killed him. Once he was dead, they put him in a tomb, but on the third day, he rose from the grave. From that time on, he has forgiven and adopted all who would believe, into the kingdom of God forever.

Lerrad was now in tears and sobbing loudly, "I'm sorry, I believe and know God is talking to me even now, that it was for me that Jesus was sacrificed and wants me to become part of his family," sobbed Lerrad.

"That's it. All you need is to believe and live your life to the service of God and his son, Jesus. It is done!" Marc then explained to Lerrad the next step was to be baptized in water as a show of faith in the life, death, and resurrection of Jesus for the redemption of sin.

Lerrad shouted out, "Oh please, I want to be baptized."

"Follow me," said Marc as he walked out of the house to the small pond.

The three, Marc, Linda, and Lerrad, were standing on the bank of the little pond. Marc said, "Come into the water with me," and Lerrad leaped into the water out of joy. Once he had composed himself, Lerrad went to where Marc was standing in water to his waist. Marc held Lerrad by the back and again asked Lerrad, "Do you believe in the son of the living God, Jesus Christ?"

Still sobbing, Lerrad said, "Yes, oh yes, I do."

Marc then looked to the sky and repeated these words, "Father God in heaven, today I bring to your throne of grace Lerrad, who has confessed his allegiance to you." Marc then looked into the eyes of Lerrad and said, "I baptize you, Lerrad, in the name of the father, the son, and the Holy Spirit." As Marc spoke these words, he submerged Lerrad completely underwater. Once he brought Lerrad out of the water, Lerrad had been transfigured into a man and was no longer a toad.

Lerrad was utterly overwhelmed with joy, speaking words of thanks and joy in a language only Lerrad could understand. Marc then repeated these words. "Lerrad, you are now in

Christ, 2 Corinthians 5:17, *Therefore, if any man be in Christ, he is a new creature: old things are passed away; behold, all things are become new."*

These words fueled the joy Lerrad experienced and caused him to become all the more animated in his praise to God. As Marc and Lerrad came out of the water, Lerrad took Marc by the hand, raising it high, speaking words of thanks to God, asking a blessing for Marc in extreme love and affection. This feeling of love and joy was beyond anything Lerrad had ever known.

It is essential to explain to you, the reader of this book, that Lerrad was always a human, yet he never felt like he was anything but a worthless toad. You may have also noticed from earlier parts of the story, Lerrad had an issue with alcohol and other substances. Mara in the story represents alcohol, Hebrew in origin, and the meaning of mara is "bitter," which carries the implication "strength." Other plants mentioned in the story are symbolic of addictive substances. Since Lerrad's spiritual experience, he has been completely healed of all desires to use substances, including alcohol. I also want to mention that Lerrad did try to quit the use of these substances beforehand yet failed on his own. It was only through a complete submission to God and the power of the Holy Spirit that Lerrad was able to be completely healed from substance abuse. The last sentence is crucial for you to understand. It is only by complete submission to God that things can change for the good. I know many people have tried to quit alcohol and other substances and have failed repeatedly. When you hear the phrase, "give it to God," it is, in reality, the only way to be completely healed. Since you have come this far with me, please continue this journey to the kingdom. It is not yet over. Let us pick up where we left off.

After a period of prayer and sobbing of joy, all three went back into the house. Now that Lerrad was filled with the spirit of God, he understood more than ever that he needed to take this journey to the kingdom. Marc brought out a Bible from another room and gave it to Lerrad, telling him, "Your journey to the kingdom of God is explained in these words. Search the scriptures diligently, know they are directions to treasures beyond anything you could understand."

After Lerrad's profound spiritual encounter, he did stay with Marc and Linda for several days. During this time, Lerrad was taught many things from the Bible. With guidance from Marc, Lerrad was able to comprehend things he did not understand on his own. After his time with Marc and Linda, Lerrad returned home to his mother and decided to attend Bible college. The lessons learned from Bible college have become vital in understanding God's will in Lerrad's life. While attending Bible college, Lerrad met Grace and found they were an excellent complement to each other. Grace and Lerrad became closer, and Lerrad received a word from God that he was to marry and take care of Grace. After Lerrad's completion of Bible college, the two were married and began working together on a ministry they share. Lerrad later continued to a chaplaincy course, and after completion, was ordained as a chaplain. Lerrad and Grace share a wonderful life and are blessed immeasurably even to this day.

Since his youth Lerrad has always been interested in motorcycles and started riding regularly. After Lerrad's marriage to Grace, he was fortunate to purchase a motorcycle, making it a small step to become a Christian Motorcyclists Association member. Following his first year as a member of the group, Lerrad was elected chaplain of the local chapter in the town he now lives.

The journey to the kingdom is not to a physical destination but a constant spiritual journey. Each day, we must continue the journey with faith and resolve to serve our Lord every step of the way. Only by the direction of God through his spirit can we know the way to the kingdom. According to Zechariah 4:6, *"Then he answered and spake unto me, saying, This is the word of the LORD unto Zerubbabel, saying, Not by might, nor by power, but by my Spirit, saith the LORD of hosts."* In addition, Matthew 19:26 says, *"But Jesus beheld them, and said unto them, With men this is impossible; but with God all things are possible."*

Are you ready for your journey to the kingdom? Ask him now and listen for the words, "follow me." According to John 8:12, *"Then spake Jesus again unto them, saying, I am the light of the world: he that followeth me shall not walk in darkness, but shall have the light of life."*

The first step in your journey to the kingdom starts by turning to the next page.

YOUR FIRST STEPS TO THE KINGDOM

I want here and now to invite you to ponder the story you just read, and I pray that if you can relate to the characters in any way (or even if you have nothing in common with Lerrad), I invite you to commit to taking the journey to the kingdom of God.

- The first step is knowing you are a sinner. Romans 3:23 states, *"For all have sinned, and come short of the glory of God."* We inherited it through Adam, we are all born into flesh.

According to John 3:6, *"That which is born of the flesh is flesh; and that which is born of the Spirit is Spirit."* And Romans 8:5 teach us, *"For they that are after the flesh do mind the things of the flesh; but they that are after the Spirit the things of the Spirit."*

- Believe that God is, and that he sent his son to forgive you. According to Romans 10:9, *"That if thou shalt confess with thy mouth the Lord Jesus, and shalt believe in thine heart that God hath raised him from the dead, thou shalt be saved."*

- Trust and believe faithfully that he will forgive you. According to 1 John 1:9, *"If we confess our sins, he is faithful and just to forgive us our sins, and to cleanse us from all unrighteousness."* In addition, John 3:16, says, *"For God so loved the world, that he gave his only begotten son, that whosoever believeth in him should not perish, but have everlasting life."*

- Ask for forgiveness. According to Romans 10:10, *"For with the heart man believeth unto righteousness; and with the mouth confession is made unto salvation."*

- Receive it. Romans 10:13 says, *"For whosoever shall call upon the name of the Lord shall be saved."*

- Continue in your quest through a relationship with God. We learn in Colossians 2:6–7 KJV *"[6] As ye have therefore received Christ Jesus the Lord, so walk ye in him: [7] Rooted and built up in him, and stablished in the faith, as ye have been taught, abounding therein with thanksgiving."*

It is essential to understand that all of this is a process and can only be taken with perseverance and fully dedicating oneself to the quest for the kingdom of heaven. One of the best things a person can do is to, as we learn from John 5:39, *"Search the scriptures; for in them ye think ye have eternal life: and they are they which testify of me."* Jesus spoke these teachings in parable form to better understand the meanings of what He was trying to teach. In Matthew 13:44–46, we see, "*[44] Again, the Kingdom of heaven is like unto treasure hid in a field; the which when a man hath found, he hideth, and for joy thereof goeth and selleth all that he hath, and buyeth that field. [45] Again, the Kingdom of heaven is like unto a merchant man, seeking goodly pearls. [46] Who, when he had found one pearl of great price, went and sold all that he had, and bought it."* From these scriptures, we can see that Christ wanted us to understand how valuable, how important, and how vital it is to sacrifice all and search out and behold the kingdom of heaven. The following teachings will help us understand a few critical things about our relationship with God.

It is not good to lead a person to the cross of Jesus (the plan of salvation) and leave them there to figure things out independently. It is crucial to disciple each new believer by the examples, trials, and errors all believers go through. It would

63

be like handing the keys to your car to a child just because he can sit in the driver's seat.

ADDITIONAL TEACHINGS

Next, we need to understand it is our job to "water our garden." If we were to plant a garden and forget to give it water, eventually it would die off. That is the same thing with our spiritual garden. We know that plants need certain things to survive, water, sunshine, nutrition, and air. Leave off even one of these, and the plants will eventually wither away.

Let us parallel that to our need to take care of our spiritual garden. Here are the things critical to spiritual growth.

- Faith, you must believe.

- Communication is extremely important. Speak to God in daily prayer, then listen for him to speak to you through his words (studying the Bible). I cannot express how vital it is to have a relationship with God through prayer and meditation on his word.

- Filled with the spirit, ask him to fill you with his spirit and believe.

- Praise

Love God and praise him often. Musical aids are a great way to emote praise. Do not be afraid to make some noise

- **FAITH**

According to Hebrews 11:6, *"But without faith it is impossible to please him: for he that cometh to God must believe that he is, and that he is a rewarder of them that diligently seek him."*

Faith of a Mustard Seed

Faith is the key that unlocks the door to change. I can run around all day long and shout and scream about the glory of God and how he is the creator of the world, yet if I do not believe it deep down in my spirit, I am just making noise.

In Hebrews chapter 11, there is an entire lesson on the topic of faith and how some of the most significant figures in the Bible succeeded because of this one act, faith. Hebrews 11:1 tells us, *"Now faith is the substance of things hoped for, the evidence of things not seen."* Take a moment and turn to Hebrews 11 and read for yourself.

We could think about this word *faith* in a couple of ways that are easy for us to understand. If I go to a light switch and flip it on, I have faith that the light will illuminate, yet if I do not believe, I probably will not even try, what would be the use? I have also heard another analogy, how do we know there is a God? By faith, we must believe, and when we do, he will let us know. If we say there is no God because we cannot see him, I can reply that I have never seen the wind, but I know it is there because I feel it. I know that God is with me because I feel his Spirit. According to Matthew 17:20, *"And Jesus said unto them, Because of your unbelief: for verily I say unto you, If ye have faith as a grain of mustard seed, ye shall say unto this mountain. Remove hence to yonder place; and it shall remove; and nothing shall be impossible unto you."*

Now I know none of us have moved any mountains in the literal sense, but we need to remember our faith is something that is practiced, and I mean it needs to be exercised every day. It is because we are not letting our spirit take control and that we are used to the natural world, yet it is not the natural we are striving to unite with. We see in Romans 8:5, *"For they that are after the flesh do mind the things of the flesh; but they that are after the Spirit the things of the Spirit."* And in Romans 8:9, *"But ye are not in the flesh, but in the Spirit, if so be that the Spirit of God dwell in you."*

Only by the Spirit of the living God can we do anything, and I mean only by his grace are we save not of our works. We need to say as the man who had the son filled with a "dumb and deaf spirit," in Mark 9:23–24, "[23] *Jesus said unto him, If thou canst believe, all things are possible to him that believeth. [24] And straightway the Father of the child cried out, and said with tears, Lord, I believe; help thou mine unbelief."*

We need to ask God for help with our faith. Our faith is even smaller than a mustard seed, and if we want it to grow, we need to exercise it daily. Do not go out and ask for a million dollars. Start small and believe with all your heart that God is a rewarder of those who diligently seek him. Believe it, receive it, and that is the final word. According to Mark 11:24, *"Therefore I say unto you, what things soever ye desire, when ye pray, believe that ye receive them, and ye shall have them."*

Go ahead and give it a try . . . I dare you.

- COMMUNICATION WITH GOD

The sweetest prayer of all

As I searched the Bible, I found many things on prayer and specifically what Jesus had to say about prayer, and that when you read the gospels through, you will find Jesus is in constant prayer with the father. It was common for Christ to sneak off and spend several hours in loving conversation with His Father.

In Matthew 14:23, *"And when he had sent the multitudes away, he went up into a mountain apart to pray: and when the evening was come, he was there alone."*

We read in Mathew 5:44, *"But I say unto you, Love your enemies, bless them that curse you, do good to them that hate you, and pray for them which despitefully use you, and persecute you."* And in Matthew 6:7, *"But when ye pray, use not vain repetitions, as the heathen do: for they think that they shall be heard for their much speaking."* He also teaches us how to pray, in Matthew 6:9, *"The Lord's prayer."* Take a look and read through this passage yourself. Go ahead, I will wait.

Continued reading of the scriptures will reveal a special prayer that needs to be understood. In John 17, Christ was praying an intense, heartfelt prayer to the father. He knew it was time for going to the cross, and his work was almost done. He was thanking the father for all that he had done for him and glorifying him in the most beautiful prayer recorded in the Bible. As it says in John 17:4–5, 8, *"[4] I have glorified thee on the earth: I have finished the work which thou gavest me to do.*

[5] And now, O Father, glorify thou me with thine own self with the glory which I had with thee before the world was. . .

[8] For I have given unto them the words which thou gavest me; and they have received them, and have known surely that I came out from thee, and they have believed that thou didst send me."

The words he spoke were like a beautiful symphony of thanksgiving, of glorification of the father, of being wholly devoted to speaking to God, thanking him for all of these things. When we get to John 17:20, *"Neither pray I for these alone, but for them also which shall believe on me through their word,"* I have to pause a minute. There is something there, did you see it? Let us read it again. Wait a minute. We believe in Jesus through the words of the disciples. Is he saying that I pray for you? That we could take it personally and put our name in place *"but for them also which shall believe on me through their word"*? Because I believe on Jesus Christ through the words of disciples. Literally, Christ Jesus said a prayer for us. That may or may not mean a lot right this second. Just read it over and let it sink in. For me, it just melted my heart as it strengthened my faith and love for Jesus all the more. Pray one for another, trust in Jesus Christ, and know that he said a special prayer just for you.

- **Read your Bible to hear from God**

If you take the words of the Bible literally and personally, it will change your life forever. Read your Bible daily. As we read in John 5:39, "Search the scriptures; for in them ye think ye have eternal life: and they are they which testify of me."

God's Love Letters

According to Hebrew 4:12, *"For the word of God is quick, and powerful, and sharper than any two-edged sword, piercing even to the dividing asunder of soul and spirit, and of the joints and marrow, and is a discerner of the thoughts and intents of the heart."* Perhaps one of the most important yet most overlooked and neglected parts of a successful relationship with God is studying the Bible. It is vital to the spiritual growth of all who believe. Somehow we need to prioritize time to study God's word. Consider Proverbs 3:1, *"My son, forget not my law; but let thine heart keep my commandments,"* and Proverbs 3:8, *"It shall be health to thy navel, and marrow to thy bones."* The Bible is a roadmap to the life Christ has set as an example. We cannot find our way to the kingdom of God without proper directions. Even a contractor needs to use a guide, "a blueprint," to be able to build a house correctly. Communication with God is not a one-sided event. We need to listen for his loving words of encouragement and compassion. I can say it a million ways, but it comes down to one thing, read your Bible daily. As we see in Joshua 1:8, *"This book of the law shall not depart out of thy mouth; but thou shalt meditate therein day and night, that thou mayest observe to do according to all that is written therein: for then thou shalt make thy way prosperous, and then thou shalt have good success."* And Psalms 1:1–2, "[1] *Blessed is the man that walketh not in the counsel of the ungodly, nor standeth in the way of sinners, nor sitteth in the seat of the scornful. [2] But his delight is in the law of the LORD; and in his law doth he meditate day and night."*

• THE HOLY SPIRIT

How To Fly Your Kite

Growing up as a young boy, it was always a fascination of mine to fly a kite. As a less-than-wealthy family member, I had learned to improvise on many occasions. At this specific time, I tried my hand at making my own kites from scratch, in other words, homemade. Obviously, the first of these prototypes was highly crude, to say the least. So, trying to fly these paperweights was less than successful in the beginning. The one thing I remember is running with all my strength to try and loft these pitiful replicas of a kite. I tried to change up the design and added tails and ribbons to stabilize with no hope for a successful launch. Eventually, it was probably from pity that someone had purchased me a kite from the store, including a spool of proper kite string. Once handed to me, I ripped the seal off of this baby as fast as I could and looked at this beautiful piece of aerodynamic wonder. I did take note of the construction and noticed that the wood pieces were made from exceptionally lightweight wood, unlike the heavy tree limbs that my homemade counterparts were crafted from. In a rush to put this kite together, it was all that I could do to contain my excitement. Finally, she was ready for flight, and out the door, I ran.

With but one thing on my mind once I had arrived at the appointed spot, I began to, as I had done before, run with all of my strength to coerce this store-bought wonder to soar like a bird. Unfortunately, this was not the case. Just like my homemade birds had done in the past, this stupid kite spun around a few times like a pinwheel and bounced to the ground with a thud. What the heck, I thought? While completely tired from running and out of breath, I gave up and went home very discouraged. Okay, fine, I was unhappy and mad at this dumb kite. It must have been a defective kite, I thought. Could it have been my gifter purchased this kite from a particular on-sale defective kite area of the store? On the next day, I was less than motivated to approach the shame of the previous day.

As time passed, I tried to re-create my efforts to ferret out any significant mistakes that I might have made. I just could not continue the process for long, as again, the pain of defeat was greater than the desire to understand the why. I was done with the whole mess. I had not noticed that as I was going through this process, I was outside. Walking through my yard and, with frustration, I kicked the ground below me and noticed something strange. When I kicked the ground, a small cloud of dust arose and was carried away by a puff of wind. This day was different than the day before. There was a light breeze that got me thinking, could it be that simple? I ran to my room and grabbed the defective kite, and out the door I went, again, to the same spot as I had the day before. This time, before I could start to run, the darn thing jerked out of my hand and was aloft before I could even figure out what was happening. Woo-hoo! I screamed as this beauty started to reach for the heavens

75

unspooling the entire roll of string. If only I had more string, I thought. Before I knew it, this defective kite was so high that I could barely see it. Joy overwhelmed me as I watched this wonder of aerodynamics and realized I did not have to run to get her up. It was the wind, and without this wind, I was wasting my time and energy. That without the wind, no amount of running was able to bring this kite to fly.

Possibly by now, you may see where I am going with this. As young Christians, we become so excited to do, to change the world, to earn and perhaps feel worthy of God's love, we try to do things of our own strength. We read the Bible, go to church, listen to praise music, and vowed never to sin again. All good things in their own right, yet before we know it, we become discouraged and tired, sometimes even giving up; we just do not get it. We might say something is missing. Well, of course, the wind, that is what is missing, the breath of God, the Holy Spirit. According to Hebrews 11:6, *"But without faith, it is impossible to please him: for he that cometh to God must believe that he is, and that he is a rewarder of them that diligently seek him."*

Through our faith, we allow his spirit to take control of us. We learn in 1 Corinthians 13:1, *"Though I speak with the tongues of men and of angels, and have not charity* (Or the love of God, His spirit), *I am become as sounding brass, or a tinkling cymbal."* Or just a hollow kite without the wind.

The efforts we put into our relationship with God are sometimes just that, our efforts. *"Strength will rise as we wait upon the Lord"* (Isaiah 40:31). Sometimes we need to *"be still and know that he is God"* (Psalms 46:10). Wait for the wind; it will come. According to Acts 1:4, *"And, being assembled together with them, commanded them that they should not depart from Jerusalem, but WAIT for the promise of the Father, which, saith he, ye have heard of me."* And Acts 2:1–4 *"[1] And when the day of Pentecost was fully come, they were all with one accord in one place. [2] And suddenly there came a sound from heaven as of a rushing mighty wind, and it filled all the house where they were sitting. [3] And there appeared*

77

unto them cloven tongues like as of fire, and it sat upon each of them. [4] And they were all filled with the Holy Ghost, and began to speak with other tongues, as the Spirit gave them utterance." The promise of Jesus Christ had come to them as he had said.

We should never get discouraged yet continue to pray and wait. As you do continue in study and prayer, go into this with the understanding that it is by the Spirit of God and not of our own works we can do these things. According to Ephesians 2:8–9, "[8] *For by grace are ye saved through faith; and that not of yourselves: it is the gift of God: [9] Not of works, lest any man should boast."*

Do not run out of breath trying to fly. Let the spirit, the breath of God, take you, and then you will fly higher than you could have ever imagined. I may have left you wondering, how do I get there? There are no secret words to recite, no magic potion. Instead, it is the idea of coming into an intimate relationship with God. Without that relationship, we are just doing it on our own. As I in my youth did struggle, become frustrated, and discouraged with the kite, we Christians can also experience the same feelings when we try to do it on our own. As we read in Romans 8:31, *"What shall we then say to these things? If God be for us, who can be against us?"*

Continue going to church. I never said that was a bad thing. Continue reading your Bible. I never said that was a bad thing either, but now go through these practices open-minded. Look for God's direction. Wait on his spirit to change you. The more you push at something or try to force it, the harder it becomes to receive that movement.

What I am saying is that sometimes we need to allow things to happen. God's peace, his spirit will overflow in us beyond what we can ever think, hope for, or imagine. When the Holy Spirit becomes part of us, it will be an experience we will understand and want to speak of and contemplate all the time. This will be like turning on a switch to a light. In summary, trust in God, seek him with your heart, with your whole heart, and you will find him. Press into a relationship with God, not as a master–servant relationship, but a loving, happy learning experience through the spirit of God. Never give up, never be discouraged, wait upon the Lord, and you will be strengthened as the eagles. God never fails.

- EXPRESSIONS OF LOVE FOR GOD (PRAISE AND WORSHIP)

With a Grateful Heart

The most important thing to remember in our life is that we are all created in the image of God, that we are fallen from the grace of God, yet through that grace, we are saved from the punishment we deserve. From the beginning, we are to walk and talk with God continually, yet through the desire of the flesh, man chose to be separated from God.

In Romans 3:23 we learn, *"For all have sinned, and come short of the glory of God; only through this next verse can we be restored into the fellowship with God."* And in Ephesians 2:8–9, *"[8] For by Grace are ye saved through faith; and that not of yourselves: it is the gift of God:[9] Not of works, lest any man should boast."*

What? You mean my works cannot buy me a spot in the kingdom of God by doing good? I know I am preaching to the choir, and that we all know this, but I need to set the stage a little, so bear with me.

We need to understand that God loves us even when we are not doing his will, that in Romans 8:38, says, *"nothing can separate us from the Love of God through Christ Jesus,"* and in Romans 5:8–9, *"[8] But God commendeth his love toward us, in that, while we were yet sinners, Christ died for us. [9] Much more than, being now justified by his blood, we shall be saved from wrath through him."* He loves us!

God loves us, and we cannot do anything to earn this love, yet when someone does something for us that we do not deserve, what do we do? We thank the person. Suppose that thing he or she did was to save our life from eternal damnation? I want you to think about that last sentence for a minute and see if it cannot stir up some emotions of gratitude and adoration for the one true God and Jesus Christ. Psalms 100:1–5 "[1] *A Psalm of praise. Make a joyful noise unto the LORD, all ye lands. [2] Serve the LORD with gladness: come before his presence with singing. [3] Know ye that the LORD he is God: it is he that hath made us, and not we ourselves; we are his people, and the sheep of his pasture. [4] Enter into his gates with thanksgiving, and into his courts with praise: be thankful unto him, and bless his name. [5] For the LORD is good; his mercy is everlasting; and his truth endureth to all generations.*"

Go into a private place and lock the door, put on some of your favorite praise music, and just let it go. Sing and shout and thank God, dance like there is no tomorrow. Be like David and just do not care what others think. According to 2 Samuel 6:14–15, "[14] *And David danced before the LORD with all his might; and David was girded with a linen ephod. [15] So David and all the house of Israel brought up the ark of the LORD with shouting, and with the sound of the trumpet.*"

Do not put it off. Do it now.

The following chapters are dedicated to further instruction in your journey to the kingdom of God. Please do not stop now, it only gets better.

FREE INDEED

Before we continue, I want it known that this message is not to make light of anyone's sickness or infirmity but rather to encourage and challenge your faith in the God who heals.

As I was pondering this message, it came to me that many people in the body of Christ have different forms of sickness and discomfort regarding the physical. We need to know more about God's will for us concerning healing, so obviously, the only place to start is the Bible. The first thing that I found that it is God who heals all our infirmities. We read in Psalms 103:2–3, "*[2] Bless the LORD, O my soul, and forget not all his benefits: [3] Who forgiveth all thine iniquities; who healeth all thy diseases.*"

Well, right there, it says that the Lord heals all diseases. Also, I remembered that when Jesus was, in Luke 2:49, *"I was about my Father's business,"* throughout the ministry of Christ he went about, *"And Jesus went about all the cities and villages, teaching in their synagogues, and preaching the gospel of the kingdom, and healing every sickness and every disease among the people"* (Matthew 9: 35). It must be God's will for us to be healed.

So now we come to the part where Jesus sent out his disciples. *"And when he had called unto him his twelve disciples, he gave them power against unclean spirits, to cast them out, and to heal all manner of sickness and all manner of disease"* (Matthew 10:1).

This made me think. These were men who all, as we know, had problems of their own, yet by the power given to them were able to accomplish this great task. Is it possible for us to have this same power to heal as given to the disciples?

I found the answer in Romans 8:10–11, "[10] *And if Christ be in you, the body is dead because of sin; but the Spirit is life because of righteousness. [11] But if the Spirit of him that raised up Jesus from the dead dwell in you, he that raised up Christ from the dead shall also quicken your mortal bodies by his Spirit that dwelleth in you."*

That means the spirit of God living in us shall quicken (excite, stir up, refresh, strengthen, invigorate, reanimate, reactivate, revive, and revitalize) your mortal bodies. "The same power that conquered the grave lives in you."

When given this message, I had on the very same day a migraine that comes to me from time to time with a severely painful neck. So, as I was studying for this and praying about it, I heard a small voice ask me, "Do you believe God can heal this?" As soon as I heard myself say yes, I do, and asked for God to heal me, the pain was gone just that quick. It all comes down to believing that Christ came to set us free and not just in the waiting around for him to come and take us home, but the here and now. He has set us free. According to John 8:32, *"And ye shall know the truth, and the truth shall make you free."* And John *8:36, "If the Son therefore shall make you free, ye shall be free indeed."*

GOD'S GRACE

In the overall spectrum of this vast universe, it is hard to imagine how really small we as humans are, yet our God has the very hairs of our head numbered. We learn in Luke 12:7, *"But even the very hairs of your head are all numbered. Fear not therefore: ye are of more value than many sparrows."*

That the creator of all can think on us, and even more than that, He loves us. The song "I Am a Friend of God" is amazing and hard to ponder. Knowing he really cares for and loves us is beyond comprehension. *"Who am I that you are mindful of me?"*

I heard it said that most of the messengers for God were misfits and reprobates, yet he called them friends. If we were to think about it, we would understand that no one except Jesus Christ was anywhere close to worthy of teaching and imputing the word of God to the world.

If we know how he loves us, it is only fitting that we drop to our knees and worship him at the very mention of his name, to think on him with every breath we take.

Sadly, we spend less and less time in communion with God and more time chasing after worldly ties. Unfortunately, this is something we are warned of in the book of Romans, *"For to be carnally minded is death; but to be spiritually minded is life and peace"* (Romans 8:6).

The name of Jesus is above all others and is the name we should ponder at every turn, yet we are so occupied that we only give bits and pieces. If we could dedicate our entire being to God, what would that look like?

I am ashamed to say that my flesh gets in the way and does not spend as much time communing with God. I get up and go to work, come home and try to rest before dinner, and save a fleeting few moments of each day to thank him before I go to sleep, and yet he still loves me, regardless. I know for a fact that by the spirit of God, he has called me to speak and preach the living gospel of Christ my king. I can never of my own give

God the praise from my lips that he deserves. How with each day, the time flickers away, yet deep in my heart, I thank God. I am grateful for all he has done for me.

As a youth, I was always rebelling and getting in trouble. The thought that I could have anything to do within the kingdom of God is, or shall I say, even be part of the love of God was incomprehensible to me. When I get into the place of communication and peace with God, I realize that I am not worthy, yet he still loves me, and his words pour through me as if they were planted there as a seed and eventually came to fruition. Consider Jeremiah 20:9, *"Then I said, I will not make mention of him, nor speak any more in his name. But his word was in mine heart as a burning fire shut up in my bones, and I was weary with forbearing, and I could not stay."*

A lot of rambling to say, it is only by the grace of God that I can do anything. Regardless of what I have done in life, in spite of it all, the spirit of God lives in me, and his love grows within my spirit. I have heard it said by some famous singer that "life is what happens while you're busy making plans." We can never understand how much God loves us, yet he does, that is if we let him, things can change within our lives if we open up our hearts and let him in to unlock the potential of our fullest extent. Yes, he loves us, and that love is what has kept this Earth from destruction for all of these years. The God of all that is and who created this universe loves us beyond all we can think or imagine.

It all comes down to one thing, the never-ending, unearned favor of God, that is right, the grace of God. Without it, we are nothing, and with it, we are everything He says we are. Stop here and read Ephesians chapter 1.

HE HEALED THEM ALL

Once, on a much-needed day off, I was led to finish up some honey-do chores, and lo and behold, I came across a stack of papers. Once I began to look through them, I found they were handwritten copies of prayer requests from our chapter meetings dating back to early 2018. What I noticed without going into a lot of detail at this time was the number of prayers with a high percentage of positive outcomes. In other words, almost all of our prayers were answered in a positive way by God himself. I also noticed that this message was a close correlation to the message he gave me for the last meeting. He had planted a seed that took root and started to grow. Here is where the word of God showed me the reason for this. To start with, one of my favorite passages is Psalms 103 1–3, "[1] *A Psalm of David. Bless the LORD, O my soul: and all that is within me, bless his holy name. [2] Bless the LORD, O my soul, and forget not all his benefits: [3] Who forgiveth all thine iniquities; who healeth all thy diseases.*"

There is more, yet I will let you go back and read the remainder of this passage for yourself for the sake of time. The main thing I want you to see is that David was praising the Lord for his forgiveness and healing. We all know that the forgiveness of sin is the key element to our salvation and our relationship with God, yet we sometimes overlook the remainder of the benefits he has to offer. Now let us fast-forward to the New Testament to see if this goes anywhere. We notice in John 5:30 Christ mentions that he only did the will of the father. *"I can of mine own self do nothing: as I hear, I judge: and my judgment is just; because I seek not mine own will, but the will of the Father which hath sent me."*

When we research the scriptures, we notice that the one thing that Christ did as he went from town to town was he healed all that would believe. There were complete regions that he traveled that he healed them all. *"And Jesus went about all the cities and villages, teaching in their synagogues, and preaching the gospel of the kingdom, and healing every sickness and every disease among the people"* (Matthew 9:35).

There you have it, and if we go back John 30, we see that Christ only did what the father told him. It must be the will of God that Jesus heals all manner of sickness. It must be the will of God that we are healed, correct?

Back to the statement about what we saw in scripture regarding the ministry of Jesus, we see that he healed the sick everywhere he went. In the same scriptures, it says that in, Hebrews 13:8, *"Jesus Christ the same yesterday, and to day, and for ever."* And in James 5:14–15, "[14] *Is any sick among you? let him call for the elders of the church; and let them pray over him, anointing him with oil in the name of the Lord. [15] And the prayer of faith shall save the sick, and the Lord shall raise him up; and if he have committed sins, they shall be forgiven him."*

Let us review. Jesus only did what his father told him, and he healed the sick, so it must be the will of the father that anyone who is sick should be healed. Does the scripture also say that Jesus Christ is the same yesterday, today, and forever? So, if it was the will of the father to heal through Jesus in the days he was in ministry on this Earth before his crucifixion, should it not also apply today?

I understand and can even be guilty of a lack of faith to be healed at times, and it is human not so much to resist, but to either feel unworthy or to not be sure that is what God wants for me. Whatever it takes to free oneself of these doubts is the key to understanding how worthy we are, that this is something we all need to hear and hear good. God loves us and has set this love in the blood of his only son, Jesus Christ. If God made such a sacrifice for us, then how can we believe anything that is not of the will of God. According to Luke 8:50, *"But when Jesus heard it, he answered him, saying, Fear not: believe only, and she shall be made whole."*

Now let us go back to the opening line of this lesson. As a collective group, God's Road Warriors have been praying for one another, and I am sure way before my time. After going back to the original prayer request (before I continue, I want you to know I take no credit other than the vessel to pray for others. It is God and God only who hears and grants our prayers, not me). With that said, I noticed that these prayers had been answered and in a positive way. It would take several pages to go over them all, and for the sake of time, I will touch on one of the more notable and profound answers to our prayers. This concerns a child, Emma, the granddaughter of members of our group. Several times we asked for healing concerning little Emma that after hearing all of the medical issues involved, it was hard not to have overwhelming compassion for her and the family. We prayed several times, and I could see in the face of the grandmother that they were very concerned and heartbroken over the original diagnosis. Then to make matters worse, their second grandchild, Stevie, was born with a cardiac issue as well.

Here is where I get to skip to the good part. God answered our prayers in this matter. On January 18 at our monthly meeting, I met both of the precious children and was amazed. Running around and playing, giggling and acting as if nothing were ever wrong. Since then, Mary sent me a text saying, at the latest doctor's visit, it has been confirmed, "The hole in Stevie's heart has closed. Emma's heart is holding its own. Stevie doesn't have to go back to the cardiologist. Emma will have to go back in a year unless we see signs of trouble." Thank you, God. Thank you, Jesus!

I want to finish with this thought. Never give up, never give in. In the words of 1 Thessalonians 5:24, *"Faithful is he that calleth you, who also will do it."*

GOD NEVER FAILS!

Knowing God

How can we explain something we know little about? It is like trying to explain the sun. We know that it is there even when we can not see it all the time, we feel its warmth, and we know of the importance it has to life on Earth. That is as close as I can come to explaining the reality of God. We know that he is and that his spirit is as essential to our life as the sun. We feel his love and warmth every time we are in his presence. Why is it then that we would hide our faces from him as if to be afraid to be burned by the sheer glory of his being? For me, it was the fear of what I was told, that God was a stern judge and that he was mad at me for not doing good or sinning as it were. I found out by his spirit telling me that was just not true, in fact, the opposite is true. He loves me no matter what I do, and his loving arms are always open to receive me in unconditional love and forgiveness. I have learned the more I seek his love, the more significant portion he has to give. It had to be about a choice for me, a choice to give up everything that I held on to that would separate me from his grace. It was actually me who

95

held back the blessings he so desired to give me. I was trying to receive his favor and did not want to give up habits that brought about a wall between him and me. It took many years of his patient loving calling to break through that wall and bring about understanding that it was my choices that separated me from the joy of the Lord.

I am not perfect in my flesh, yet my spirit is complete and filled with his love. This is a love that surpasses all understanding, even the glory of the living God and Jesus Christ. The next thing I needed to understand was that it was my job to seek him daily and to have a greater understanding of him and his love for me. I needed to realize that the enemy would not give up without a fight, and I needed to have the tools to win each battle. I can do no good in my flesh, yet through the power of the Holy Spirit, I am more than a conquer. I am a new creature in Christ. Each day is now a joy, and the love of God pours out on and through me as a mighty rushing river. I cannot hold it in, nor do I wish to, knowing it is

God's plan for his light to shine through me, and if I reject that love, it will not serve his purpose in my life.

SEVEN SECONDS TO MIDNIGHT

It is so apparent that time is the enemy of all humanity. When you start off in life, there are no user manuals or way of knowing. The farther you go, the harder it becomes to deal with this age-old enemy, time.

We think we have it all together, and we believe things will get done in their due time. The next thing you know, there is no more. You have run out of time. An interesting subject, to say the least, the thoughts that brought me to this place are, of course, the same subject. While looking at the calendar, I realized that if I did not sit down and word this out, I would have run out of time and missed the deadline.

Perhaps the other reason I was directed to plan this topic around time is, recently, I was honored to speak in front of a group of prisoners at the territorial prison in Cannon City. It is hard not to think of what these men must be going through, and as it turns out, most of them have plenty of time. Will they make good use of the time they have or not? As a member of the prison ministries team, I would like to think that we had at least touched a handful of hearts.

Even if you think you have all the time in the world, it will always never be enough. The truth is, time is running out. In the Bible, there is a quote from Christ himself that says, *"Behold, I come as a thief. Blessed is he that watcheth, and keepeth his garments, lest he walk naked, and they see his shame* (Revelation 16:15). Further, *"But of that day and hour knoweth no man, no, not the angels of heaven, but my Father only"* (Matthew 24:36).

We will be going along as if nothing is happening and "Wammo" time has ran out. "[38] *For as in the days that were before the flood they were eating and drinking, marrying and giving in marriage, until the day that Noe entered into the ark, [39] And knew not until the flood came, and took them all away; so shall also the coming of the Son of man be"* (Matthew 24:38–39).

I know that most of us are aware of the fleeting time, and as Christians, I hope we are all ready for the coming of the king, because like it or not the time is coming faster than we think, and then we will stand before him and here these words "[34] *Then shall the King say unto them on his right hand, Come, ye blessed of my Father, inherit the kingdom prepared for you from the foundation of the world. [35] For I was an hungred, and ye gave me meat: I was thirsty, and ye gave me drink: I was a stranger, and ye took me in: [36] Naked, and ye clothed me: I was sick, and ye visited me: I was in prison, and ye came unto me. [37] Then shall the righteous answer him, saying, Lord, when saw we thee an hungred, and fed thee? or thirsty, and gave thee drink? [38] When saw we thee a stranger, and took thee in? or naked, and clothed thee? [39] Or when saw we thee sick, or in prison, and came unto thee? [40] And the King shall answer and say unto them, Verily I say unto you, Inasmuch as ye have done it unto one of the least of these my brethren, ye have done it unto me*" (Matthew 25:34–40).

Because *"That at the name of Jesus every knee should bow, of things in heaven, and things in earth, and things under the earth; 11 And that every tongue should confess that Jesus Christ isLord, to the glory of God the Father"* (Philippians 2:10).

"TICK TOCK."

WHAT ARE WE THINKING?

When we look around and ponder the overall state of the Earth, the one thing that comes to the mind of all intelligent creatures is this world has changed for the worse. It is like some of us have lost our minds. Constant bickering and destruction of everything we hold dear. All that we have been taught as suitable has now been turned around and looked on as wrong. What we know as evil and wicked are now acceptable. What is good and pure is considered wrong. Hatred and horrendous sin are entirely accepted and even taught as the expected behavior of this society. It is up to us as Christians to stand the moral high ground regardless of anything that goes on around us, yet do we? Know that we are living in the end times, that we live in the prophesied world spoken of in the Bible.

The problem is this: we have all gone so blind, and if not blind complacent, apathetic to what is going on around us. We feel that if something does not immediately impact us, we can overlook it. The sad reality is that these things will continue to grow and affect every human being in one way or another (if it has not already). We need to stand up as a united front, put on the armor of God, hold true to what we believe, and understand that nothing is going to change unless we change it. Things will only get worse. Our political leaders, try as some may, are bombarded on every issue and forced to make certain compromises to keep the majority appeased. Arguing, infighting, and disregard for anything true and good, is now the new normal. This may sound like a litany of the same words spoken repeatedly, yet the reality is unless we do our part, nothing will ever change. By God's grace, we carry his name, yet if we believe we can just sit down and watch this play out this is a dangerous mindset indeed. We must fight, and we need to teach our children to fight as well. I do not mean the physical schoolyard fighting. I mean to stand up for what is right all the time, to speak out continually against injustice and the demoralization of this world. "Onward Christian soldiers marching as to war." Words from a song taught in the church need to be our battle cry, hold our Bibles in the air, and shout "This is how I fight my battles," with the sword of the Lord our God.

I heard an analogy once that will fit right in. If we know a poisonous snake is living under our bed, would we just let it alone and hope he does not crawl into bed with us? Why do we feel that the poison of this world will not affect us if we just sit back and watch it play out? Now is the time. We need Jesus more than ever. We need to get up and dress for battle, and if we do not do something, what will be the outcome? Are we willing to let the snake live under our bed?

THE BATTLE AGAINST DARKNESS

As I set here on this Memorial Day, I find it more than fitting that we bow our heads in a prayer of gratitude to the men and women who gave their all for the freedom of this great nation. I did not have the privilege to serve in the military but know many who have, and find they all have one thing in common, the love for the freedom of the United States of America. If you ask any one of the fine soldiers of this country, they will tell you they are and always will be willing to sacrifice their life for this great nation. For this, I am grateful beyond words and realize that this goes hand in hand with the scripture in John, *"Greater love hath no man than this, that a man lay down his life for his friends"* (John 15:13).

We must also remember that beyond the battlefields abroad, we also fight against the same enemy every day, *"For we wrestle not against flesh and blood, but against principalities, against powers, against the rulers of the darkness of this world, against spiritual wickedness in high places"* (Ephesians 6:12).

Would a good soldier go into battle without the proper gear? Not going to happen! "[10] *Finally, my brethren, be strong in the Lord, and in the power of his might. [11] Put on the whole armour of God, that ye may be able to stand against the wiles of the devil. [12] For we wrestle not against flesh and blood, but against principalities, against powers, against the rulers of the darkness of this world, against spiritual wickedness in high places. [13] Wherefore take unto you the whole armour of God, that ye may be able to withstand in the evil day, and having done all, to stand. [14] Stand therefore, having your loins girt about with truth, and having on the breastplate of righteousness; [15] And your feet shod with the preparation of the gospel of peace; [16] Above all, taking the shield of faith, wherewith ye shall be able to quench all the fiery darts of the wicked. [17] And take the helmet of salvation, and the sword of the Spirit, which is the word of God: [18] Praying always with all prayer and supplication in the Spirit, and watching thereunto with all perseverance and supplication for all saints"* (Ephesians 6:10–18). Suit up and get ready. Things may get ugly.

THE BEST THINGS IN LIFE

Usually, when I try to develop a topic for these articles, the ones that bring about the most passion are the things or issues that are the most personal to me. The inspiration for this particular piece was inspired by a movie I had recently viewed in which a young man was obsessed with trying to become wealthy and worked hard at everything he did to accomplish this goal. By the end of the movie, it was apparent that the things that meant the most to him (his family and happiness) were in severe neglect. As you can already guess, in the end, he had figured out that all his wealth could not bring him the happiness he had in his family. In comparison to my life, when I think about essential things, even though it seems to be a series of running around chasing after financial comfort, what matters the most are the things I already have. A warm house, a full refrigerator, employment that allows me to continue, and a wonderful wife who takes excellent care of me. I am truly blessed.

In the scriptures, Christ mentions in Matthew 6:*33 "But seek ye first the kingdom of God, and his righteousness; and all these things shall be added unto you."* When I put this scripture in line with God's blessings in my life, the results are astonishing. When I run around in circles on my own and do things my way, I can get things done, but when I put God in front, the contrast is overwhelming. You see, *"I can do all things through Christ which strengtheneth me"* (Philippians 4:13). And when I trust in Christ, the magic happens. The blessings of God are Yes and Amen. *"But my God shall supply all your need according to his riches in glory by Christ Jesus"* (Philippians 4:19).

Where I am headed with this is, we have so many distractions that we often take some things for granted and lose focus on the things that matter the most. One of the things I used to like when I was younger was to walk down the banks of a creek or a small river. The things I would see made it clear to me that there is a God. The beauty of nature is God's way of blessing us with a simple thing. Not to slight the creations of God, yet engaging in this activity was a no-frills needed, simple item that was only possible through the love of our God. Since I started the story of walking down creeks, I must share one unique instant. At our family reunion a few years ago, I was able to find a trail alongside a water runoff, not very deep yet carved out a path I could traverse. It went up a slight incline, and once I had reached the top, there was a large tree down in the way. I started to climb over the fallen tree and turned my head to suddenly lock eyes with a rather large male deer and his mate. I could not have been more than eight feet from them. My emotions went from fear to complete awe of how beautiful he was, while also feeling the mutual respect our eyes were sharing. He made no threatening gesture, and I slowly turned away to give them peace. That incident only lasted a few seconds, yet I can remember every detail as if it were yesterday.

In close, I just want to say we should all take the time to meditate on the things that God has done for us and reminisce on sweet memories. The first time I held my daughter, going to a baseball game with a bunch of rowdy boys, or just spending time enjoying a cup of coffee with my wife. I know that because God loves us so much that there are better days ahead and that we will be blessed beyond anything we can imagine. "*[20] Now unto him that is able to do exceeding abundantly above all that we ask or think, according to the power that worketh in us, [21] Unto him be glory in the church by Christ Jesus throughout all ages, world without end. Amen*" (Ephesians 3:20–21).

THE CRY OF MY HEART

What can bring about thoughts of joy to a person? In this present time we live in, there are so many distractions, it is hard to imagine that we can find joy in so many things and most of them the wrong thoughts. I am in the process of turning my thoughts to the joy that is given to me by God. Let me explain this a little clearer. We need to tune our minds into the thoughts of Jesus. Suppose we let the things of the world take place in our most inner being. That is what will control us. There are verses in the Bible that talk about the glory of placing our thoughts on him. When we praise God, there is a magic that happens inside our being. Hallelujah and sing to the Lord with all that we are and can bring out. Whatever we think about is what we will become. When we think about the love of God and think about him, often we will also know that he hears us and knows the love of our heart in his presence and therefore fills us with an everlasting love and desire of our hearts.

I know I went a little off the track but let me explain. We have more control over our thoughts than we think. For instance, as we drive a car, we can be talking with someone else and driving the vehicle. We can get to our destination by muscle memory, and sometimes we do not even know how we got there. We have done it so often that we allow a part of our brain to do amazing things without even thinking about it. So now, let us take this to our relationship with God. What if we were to give all of our thoughts entirely to God for an extended time? Most of us men are analytical, and perhaps we should turn this into an experiment. To start, we would need a plan. Let us say we put together a map of sorts and think hard about what could put us in a parallel position to constantly think about and live for the God who loves us?

First, we will need a map or global positioning device. How about, for now, we use the Bible and see what we can glean from this? Let us enter into the presence of God boldly on our knees, ask for the power of God to overwhelm us, and give us the direction we need to get to where he wants us to be. Go to a private place and ask him to provide you with the direction. Now go to the Bible and search the scriptures, for in them he will speak to you. Find the scriptures that talk to you the most and meditate on them day and night. Shout out his name and praise him in spirit and truth. In all that you do, put him first. Turn off any distracting devices, even the television. Put on some of your favorite praise music, and just soak in his presence. I know for some this sounds a little dramatic, but the question is, how much do you want to know him? Sure we are all forgiven by the blood of Jesus and are in the lamb's book of life. What about while we are here waiting to be called home? Do we want to just exist, or do we want to feel the Love of God in our hearts and minds on a continual plain? God wants to spend time with us and rejoices when we seek him, and that is the main thing we should be doing. We can be like a group of followers of man and know about God, or we can experience him intimately. If we say we love him and have not the spirit of love within us, we are not of him. Jesus Christ came to change us and to place a bridge between the fallen man and the holiness of God. I implore you to seriously think about your part of the relationship with God. When we are in any relationship, it will soon fade away if we do not nurture that relationship. I know this is a simple analogy. If we have a plant and forget to water it, it will soon wilt and die. Be serious about your relationship with God. Your life depends on it, literally.

THE ELEPHANT IN THE ROOM

When I was very young, my family went to church regularly. One day the soothing music of the alter call stirred my heart, and I could not hold back. Running to the altar with tears in my eyes, I was taught to say the sinner's prayer and gave my life to Jesus Christ. At that moment, I knew I was saved, then told that I was going to heaven, now go and sin no more. That worked for a short time. I became so overwhelmed with the phrase "go and sin no more," that was all I could think about. I was not supposed to sin anymore. Easier said than done, I found out. Let us try an experiment, and see where it leads us. I want you to think of an elephant, you know, the giant animal with a long trunk and wrinkled skin. That is right, an elephant. Can you see it? Now I want you to forget about the elephant and let us go on. Do not think about the elephant from here on. Some of you have probably played this game before and know how hard it will be to forget about the elephant, but give it a try anyway.

The harder I tried not to sin, the more I learned I could not, not sin, which frustrated me so much that it caused me to think of it as an unachievable goal. What was the use anyway. I was dammed to hell. This opened the door to all kinds of things and brought about a sense of hopelessness, depression, and despair. I tried going back to church and doing the go upfront thing again in hopes that I would find something I had missed. I read my Bible and listened to the sermons, and all I heard was "blah blah blah." I did not understand any of it, and no one was trying to explain it to me. It was like they thought that everyone should just read the Bible and go to church until it would rub off or a magic lightbulb would come on inside my head. But that never happened.

Years went by, and age caught up with me. I was in such despair that I tried to reach out for help. I met a couple who had a ministry of support, and they again prayed with me, and I asked for that forgiveness from Jesus. I told them how this was the same as when I was younger. They told me not this time, "We will work with you and explain the things you don't understand." They took me to the very beginning, the cross of Jesus. We went through line by line, and they showed me how no one could ever love me the way that Christ does and that his love could never go away. These people began to disciple me as though I was part of their family, and for the first time in my life, I started to understand the love of God and how important it was to be part of a family filled with unconditional love.

I was still a little shaky at first, almost like a newborn animal trying to get on its feet for the first time. As the days went on, with the proper teaching, I began to grow. (Here is where I want to pause and make a comparison.) When I was younger and led to the cross, I was left there to fend for myself and, as I stated, told to read my Bible and study the scriptures taught in sermons. How many of you today can understand and explain the prophecies of Daniel? Or know what the items of the tabernacle and Ark of the Covenant are and what they represent? Like sending a five-year-old to high school, no wonder, I got frustrated.

After careful nurturing, my spirit became stronger, and while in prayer, one day, the Holy Spirit of the living God came to me and filled me with such joy and understanding that I could not shut up. It was like a river of words flowing out of me. At that time, I was given an understanding of the purpose God had for me and the knowledge that as a father forgives his son for mistakes, He loves me so much that nothing I can do will stop that love. That is why this passage from the Bible means so much to me and why you will hear me quote it often.

[38] *For I am persuaded, that neither death, nor life, nor angels, nor principalities, nor powers, nor things present, nor things to come, [39] Nor height, nor depth, nor any other creature, shall be able to separate us from the love of God, which is in Christ Jesus our Lord.* (Romans 8:38–39)

Does this mean that I can go and sin all I want because God will forgive me every time? *"What then? shall we sin, because we are not under the law, but under grace? God forbid."* (Romans 6–15). Let us sum it up. God loves us unconditionally, and that means even though we cannot stop thinking about sinful things, he still loves us. "[8] *For by grace are ye saved through faith; and that not of yourselves: it is the gift of God: [9] Not of works, lest any man should boast"* *(Ephesians 2:8–9).* That I cannot earn God's favor, and it is my sinful nature that is the reason for the blood of Christ. I am a child of God bought for with a precious price, the blood of Jesus. We also need to understand that as we lead the new believer to Christ, we also take the time to disciple them and lead them on the path to an understanding of God. Maybe we should think of them as little children that have not learned how to do and understand the things of an adult. Would you hand your car keys to a five-year-old child and tell him or her to go to the store for you? In the words of 1 Corinthians 13:11, *"When I was a child, I spake as a child, I understood as a child, I thought as a child: but when I became a man, I put away childish things."*

I believe we should take the time to disciple everyone we come in contact with, especially newborn Christians, to find out what they may need and what they may or may not understand. You may be saving them from years of confusion and frustration. Never assume that everyone knows how to live the life of a Christian. Do you remember the animal I said to forget?

THE KING IS COMING

For many years man has waited and watched for the second coming of Christ. Some are even bold enough to predict the date to no avail. The scriptures also tell us to know that *"no man knows the hour except the Father."* This, I believe, has set a precedent of apathy, even among Christians. The fact remains that if we believe the Bible's words, one thing is clear, the king himself, Jesus Christ, is coming back to take us home one day. According to Philippians 2:10–11, "[10] *That at the name of Jesus every knee should bow, of things in heaven, and things in earth, and things under the earth; [11] And that every tongue should confess that Jesus Christ is Lord, to the glory of God the Father."*

The scriptures also remind us that we are to be vigilant, to watch and pray: *"Watch and pray, that ye enter not into temptation: the spirit indeed is willing, but the flesh is weak"* (Matthew 26:41). *"Blessed are those servants, whom the lord when he cometh shall find watching: verily I say unto you, that he shall gird himself, and make them to sit down to meat, and will come forth and serve them"* (Luke 12:37). And *"Be ye therefore ready also: for the Son of man cometh at an hour when ye think not"* (Luke 12:40).

We know he is coming, yet go about our lives as if we have nothing but time. This was also prophesized in Matthew 24:38–39, "[38] *For as in the days before the flood, they were eating and drinking, marrying and giving in marriage, until the day that Noah entered the ark, [39] and did not know until the flood came and took them all away, so also will the coming of the Son of Man be."*

The point I am trying to make is that Christ is coming again. Whether we are looking to it or not, we will all be caught off guard. Is that a bad thing? Not necessarily, as long as we are doing the work of the master. No, we do not have to work for our salvation, yet once we are sealed with the spirit of Christ, he asks us to do a few things for him. Be mindful of the things he spoke about while on this earth, especially about how we treat others. His new commandment to us was to love one another as we love our self. In the book of James, it says that *"pure religion and undefiled before God and the Father is this, to visit the fatherless and widows in their affliction, and to keep himself unspotted from the world"* (James 1:27).

The best thing I can say is to search the scriptures and read for yourself what we are supposed to be doing as we watch and pray for the coming of our Lord. Then we will say, *"He which testifieth these things saith, Surely I come quickly. Amen. Even so, come, Lord Jesus"* (Revelation 22:20).

THE LOVE OF THE FATHER

It is amazing how when you are meditating on God, "Boom," out of nowhere, he brings you a word that shakes you to the core. We all know that God loves us and will always forgive us, but can we relate, or can we comprehend a parallel to this love? The answer can be found in the book of Luke (chapter 15). I believe by reading the entire chapter, it will open the door to answer these questions. Let us look at the first parable in this inciteful chapter.

He (Jesus) starts by relating to something they were all familiar with, raising flocks. That if a good shepherd were to lose even one of his sheep, he would leave the ninety-nine to go looking for that lost sheep. There are many things to consider here, including the safety of the ninety-nine left to fend for themselves, yet go on we must. After finding the lost sheep, there is much rejoicing. Then Jesus goes on to compare that joy to the joy in Heaven over one sinner that repents and returns over ninety-nine just or upright persons

This chapter is so full of joy that it will take more time than I initially thought. Christ then compares that same joy to a woman losing a piece of silver (coin) and searching diligently until she finds it. She is so happy she calls her friends to rejoice with her. The same comparison is made to the repentance of one sinner in Heaven. They have a party in heaven every time a sinner returns to the arms of the father. I have not even gotten to the more recognizable parable yet. Hold on, here we go . . .

This parable is in Luke 15:11–32, the parable of the prodigal son. There is so much to see here that it needs to be read several times to unpack it all. To start with, a man had two sons, the younger wanted to cash out the inheritance due him. In other words, he was in a hurry to grow up and felt he did not need the father any longer. The father allowed the son to have his share and let him go (free will). After leaving, the son blew all of his money on riotous (wasteful living). This is where the word prodigal comes from

After spending all that he has, left broke and alone, as the previous verse mentions, he was a long way from home. Undoubtedly, he was too ashamed to go running back home. The scripture continues that he was so desperate, he took work feeding pigs. He became so hungry that he was asking for the cobs from the pigs, and "no man gave unto him." What shame and stubbornness he must have experienced until he could not take it anymore, he thinks to himself, even my father's servants eat better. He decides to go back to his father. This part is essential to note.

He reasons in his heart, he would say unto the father (Confession) "I have sinned against heaven, and before thee." Unfortunately, many of us are guilty of putting off repentance until we are at the end of our rope. *"I am no longer worthy to be called thy son, make me as one of thy hired servants."* Complete and total repentance is in the deepest of meaning. He was sorry for what he had done and ready to ask forgiveness. This part always chokes me up. When he was going home yet while *"he was a far way off, his Father saw him, and has compassion, and ran, and fell on his neck, and kissed him."* Did you get the part where the father saw him a great way off? The father was undoubtedly brokenhearted when the son left and was looking, praying, and hoping the son would return each day. You need to remember this is Jesus telling a story of the joy in heaven over returning sinners, children of God. He is watching and waiting daily for the return of his beloved children. The story goes on to tell how the father called for the servants to bring *"the best robe, and put on him and a ring on his hand and shoes on his Feet . . . bring the fatted calf let us eat and be merry."* They threw a party, and were filled with overwhelming joy at the return of the son. Oh, the joy to know God loves us so much that nothing we can do can separate us from his great love. Read Romans 8:38–39. The end of this parable talks about the elder son returning from the field. He hears the party, and would not even go inside he was so angry.

He asks the father, what is this? My brother goes off and spends his inheritance with harlots and drunkenness, he comes home, and you throw him a party. For me you would not even kill a young goat that I can have a party with my friends. He was jealous. The father tells the elder son, *"you are with me always and everything I have is yours."* We should make merry and be glad. Your brother was dead and is alive again, was lost, and now is found.

Joy unspeakable and full of glory is the return of one sinner to the presence of God. He is constantly looking for his children to return to the fold. We need to take heed and not run from God but toward him. His arms are always open and ever ready to forgive and beyond that, to put the finest robe, the ring, and complete blessing. He does not care where we have been or what we have done. Once forgiven, we need to go and bid those invited to come to the arms of forgiveness.

In other words, when one of the children is lost, he has commissioned us to bring to him that which was lost, that there may be much joy and celebrating in the presence of the one and only true God. He who has been forgiven much doth love much. We do not serve God to become forgiven. That has already been done in Christ on Calvary. We serve God because we Love him. "Don't run from the Father; run to Him." He is watching for your return.

THE OPENED BOOK

Is he not wonderful? The God of all creation, ruler of all universes, who is all in all, who was and is to come. With all the power and majesty of this awesome being, he took the time to leave us, humans, a roadmap to him and his place of eternal peace and happiness. Yes, I am talking about the life-changing, everlasting, infallible word of our living God.

From the very beginning, it was and always will be his desire to communicate with us. In the garden, it was God who sought after his most incredible creation. He loves us, and even when we did not deserve to be part of his kingdom, he made the ultimate sacrifice for us to become one with him again.

Now that we set the stage, let us go for a brief tour of these beautiful words. As we know, it takes a lifetime to understand all that God has left us in his words, yet there is one theme that comes true no matter who you are and how far down the path of sin we have fallen. He loves us. He wants us to be the image of himself and to love one another. According to Genesis 1:27,

"So God created man in his own image, in the image of God created he him; male and female created he them."

We all know the rest of the story about how sin entered the Earth. We, the crown jewel of his creation, became filled with sin and hatred toward each other, that the whole world was filled with the men of exceeding wickedness, yet he still loves us. *"But God commendeth his love toward us, in that, while we were yet sinners, Christ died for us"* (Romans 5:8).

Wait, I missed something. In this wonderful book we hold so dear is a verse that changed everything, the first verse we probably learned in Sunday school as a youth: *"For God so loved the world, that he gave his only begotten Son, that whosoever believeth in him should not perish, but have everlasting life"* (John 3:16).

This son of the everlasting God, treated in ways we can not imagine. His life on earth was the magnification of the love of our God. He healed the sick, raised the dead, wept over the state of man. *"And when he was come near, he beheld the city, and wept over it"* (Luke 19:41*). "For we have not a high priest* *which cannot be touched with the feeling of our infirmities; but was in all points tempted like as we are, yet without sin"* (Hebrews 4:15).

He was treated worse than we can imagine, yet he still loves us. His ministry always had a familiar ring to it: love one another. *"A new commandment I give unto you, That ye love one another; as I have loved you, that ye also love one another"* (John 13:34).

If we remember every line in the Bible, we should adhere to this verse the most because he loves us and wants us to love as he loves us. The sermon on the mount is laid out in a way that no other passage of the Bible can explain this, and the best part, it is all in red. Matthew 5–7, check it out for yourself.

There is so much about the word of God I could say, and it would take volumes more than this one article. I will leave you with these final thoughts from Hebrews 4:12 *"For the word of God is quick, and powerful, and sharper than any two-edged sword, piercing even to the dividing asunder of soul and spirit, and of the joints and marrow, and is a discerner of the thoughts and intents of the heart."*

The word of God is alive. It knows what you need before you open the first page. Have you ever gone to the Bible, and once you read a passage, thought to yourself, "Wow, that's exactly what I needed to hear." Happy accident? I think not. "*[29] Are not two sparrows sold for a farthing? and one of them shall not fall on the ground without your Father. [30] But the very hairs of your head are all numbered. [31] Fear ye not therefore, ye are of more value than many sparrows"* (Mathew 10:29–31). Remember, God loves us so much. We are bought with the precious blood of Christ.

TRUST AND OBEY

"*[5] Trust in the LORD with all thine heart; and lean not unto thine own understanding. [6] In all thy ways acknowledge him, and he shall direct thy paths. [7] Be not wise in thine own eyes: fear the LORD, and depart from evil* (Proverb 3:5–7).

I remember this Bible verse from when I was a child going to Sunday school. It was one of the first lines of scripture I was taught to memorize, and even though these words are in my heart, I must confess, I have a way of leaning into my own understanding from time to time and feel that I am wise in my own eyes. The way we travel through this world waiting for Jesus to take us home is filled with many different weeds that can choke out the word. It is easy to become distracted and take our eyes off of God. But the one thing I have always found true is that no matter how far I wander, Jesus Christ will always pull me back when I turn to his word and trust in him. As the prodigal son returned, I know so does my heart to the pleading of Jesus Christ. Things are the way they are, and sometimes it is best to understand and never give up. Trust in God, believe with all of your heart, and he will direct your paths.

With nothing else that I do, it is God that I serve, and from time to time, I have to listen and allow his spirit to free me from my own understanding. From the old Hymn, I first sang as a youth:

> When we walk with the Lord, in the light of His word, what a glory He sheds on our way! Let us do His good will; He abides with us still, and with all who will trust and obey. Trust and obey, for there's no other way To be happy in Jesus, but to Trust and obey.

WITH GOD WITHOUT GOD

What can I say to explain the glory of God? How can we even comprehend the things that he has done for us? Even when we are not noticing what God is doing for us, he is always there for us. The scriptures say, *"I will never leave thee nor forsake thee."*

When I was younger, it was a continual struggle to get things done right, and I often wonder if there was a God and if there is, why was life so hard for me? Besides making wrong choices, I believe it comes down to maturity. The longer we do something, the better we get at doing it. In other words, practice makes perfect. *"When I was a child, I spake as a child, I understood as a child, I thought as a child: but when I became a man, I put away childish things"* (1 Corinthians 13:11).

The things of God made sense to me in a new and exciting way. I realized (and this is the critical part for me) the less I tried to do things myself, and the more I let him do, the better things worked out. The one constant is God. With him, I am everything. Without him, I am nothing.

I have learned that God likes to hear from me, and he loves to hear me say good things about him or praise him if you will. The more I focused on God, the easier it is to recognize his spirit working in my life. "[9] *But ye are not in the flesh, but in the Spirit, if so be that the Spirit of God dwell in you. Now if any man have not the Spirit of Christ, he is none of his. [10] And if Christ be in you, the body is dead because of sin; but the Spirit is life because of righteousness. [11] But if the Spirit of him that raised up Jesus from the dead dwell in you, he that raised up Christ from the dead shall also quicken your mortal bodies by his Spirit that dwelleth in you"* (Romans 8:9–11). I had to look up that word quicken in the dictionary, and when I did, it made even more sense.

> Quicken defined: (Not the tax program) stimulate or become stimulated. "Her interest quickened."
>
> Synonyms: stimulate, excite, stir up, arouse, awaken, or to be alive, to be lifted, to increase.

If we want to say it another way, the more we allow the spirit to become our identity, to rule and do his goodwill in our lives, the more alive and complete we become, *"I can do all things through Christ which strengtheneth me"* (Philippians 4:13).

Doesn't that make you want to shout and sing out the praises in the name of the one and true living God and Jesus Christ who is doing a great thing in our life? Can I get an Amen?

THE LEAST OF THESE

This week my brother and I visited two fellow riders and family at Memorial Hospital, both from different parts of the country with different things going on. We went to minister to them and found we were the ones being ministered to by God through them. I want to emphasize that we should never forget our responsibility to go to hospitals, care centers, and prisons. Where there is a need, we should fill it. If you are driving down the road and see a man standing there with a sign saying "I'm hungry," do not think to yourself, it's just a scam, think, that could be a chance for me to minister to this person. Give a couple of dollars in your pocket. What is the harm? Even if he does go out and buy alcohol or drugs, at least you know it will give you the chance to plant a seed, as you hand the money off "in Jesus' name I bless you" and know that whatsoever you do to the least of these you have done unto him.

[34] *Then shall the King say unto them on his right hand, Come, ye blessed of my Father, inherit the kingdom prepared for you from the foundation of the world: [35] For I was an*

hungred, and ye gave me meat: I was thirsty, and ye gave me

drink: I was a stranger, and ye took me in: [36] Naked, and ye

clothed me: I was sick, and ye visited me: I was in prison, and

ye came unto me. [37] Then shall the righteous answer him,

saying, Lord, when saw we thee an hungred, and fed thee? or

thirsty, and gave thee drink? [38] When saw we thee a

stranger, and took thee in? or naked, and clothed thee? [39]

Or when saw we thee sick, or in prison, and came unto thee?

[40] And the King shall answer and say unto them, Verily I say

unto you, Inasmuch as ye have done it unto one of the least of

these my brethren, ye have done it unto me. (Matthew 25:34–

40)

SHATTERED VESSELS

There is a Japanese form of art called kintsugi, where broken

pottery is put back together with a unique mixture that

incorporates gold or silver (usually gold) to put the vessel back

together. Once this process is finished, the outcome becomes a

work of art second to none, making the finished work more

beautiful than the original. Some pieces of this pottery are extremely valuable.

Jeremiah chapter 18 talks about comparing a potter and the clay, how the potter, when noticing an imperfection in his work, can rework the clay and turn it again into a perfect piece. This is not the exact same thing as the kintsugi, but similarity does derive from this biblical quote. We have all at one point in our lives felt the reworking of our being by the mighty hands of God. There are those of us who have been shattered to pieces in more ways than others. This world is full of those who are destructive and hasten the pain and displacement of those broken pieces, causing a great need for the gentle, loving hands of God in their lives.

I know that some of us have had a fairly good life and probably have not strayed far from the goodness of Christian life. Without much firsthand knowledge in the realm of shattered lives, that is not to say that we had not had issues or problems that took the mighty hand of God to restore us to a more normal place than we were when we started. Regardless of who we are and what we have done, there are people who have helped in one way or another. I would like to believe that as a member of the Christian Motorcyclists Association, we have been called to make a difference in the lives of those who have been broken and or shattered.

Now let us go back to the kintsugi. As we go through the direction of our living God, have been inserted into the lives of others, usually, we do not know how badly shattered those fragile lives have become. We are now incorporated into those lives, and the love of God, through us has made a way to transfer them into a more perfect and beautiful person. We are now as the gold inserted into the shattered vessels, and have been merged into those we sometimes only encounter for a very short time yet make a profound impression on them. We need to know that as we go about the highways and byways doing our thing, that there are more shattered pieces than we can imagine, that as we go, we need to in our hearts understand that even the short visit of time can make a significant impact on someone's life. As the love of God incorporates every human vessel, each piece is carefully mended back together with a profound beauty second to none. Ending with this last thought, be sure that everywhere we go, we reflect the will, desire, and love of our God. Good or bad, we can make an impression on people. We may or may not do things that could influence somebody in the wrong way. Not to say we are all problem causers, yet sometimes we need to watch the things we say and do. It is our responsibility through the grace of God to mend these shattered vessels into a priceless one of a kind piece treasured in the eyes of God.

WHAT DO WE VALUE

What is our most valuable possession? I heard it asked once to imagine your house was on fire. What would be the first thing you would rescue? I know that is an extreme exaggeration, yet it makes you think. What is truly important to us? I will not continue by disclosing what I would rescue, but to say, as I pondered what I could not do without, my family and friends come to mind first. Let us take that a bit further. I live in a fourplex and have neighbors above and next door to me. The word of God came to me that says, to *"Love the Lord God with all your heart and Love your neighbor as yourself."* (Luke 10:27)

I do have to admit that my neighbors do some things that annoy me, yet when it comes down to it, I will sacrifice my safety to make sure they were safely out of danger. It also occurred to me, I do love my neighbors, but maybe not as I love myself. What I mean is, I would go out of my way to protect them from emanating danger, yet when was the last time I spoke to any of them? When God brings about reminders and reflections of our actions or inactions regarding our acquaintances, it is not to condemn us but to remind us that we must care for each other. This care for one another needs to be in a way that is equal or greater than what we do for ourselves. This is a hard pill to swallow, but if we *"do unto these the least of these,"* God has likened our actions to how we treat him and that we will be blessed and inherit the kingdom of God when we treat others with compassion. Or the opposite, when we do nothing to comfort the least of these, "[45] *Then shall he answer them, saying, Verily I say unto you, Inasmuch as ye did it not to one of the least of these, ye did it not to me. [46] And these shall go away into everlasting punishment: but the righteous into life eternal"* (Matthew 25:45–46). Stop what you are doing right now, reach out to your neighbor or someone you can call, and say, I thought about you and wanted to know if you are okay. Do you need anything I can help with?

If we as Christians will reread the scriptures, we can see that God has a specific plan of treating each other. Christ himself spoke openly about the importance of treating others with compassion and love. "[9] *And let us not be weary in well doing: for in due season we shall reap, if we faint not. [10] As we have therefore opportunity, let us do good unto all men, especially unto them who are of the household of faith"* (Galatians 6:9–10).

I hope you have enjoyed your journey up to now. I invite you to reread passages of this text, always asking for the spirit of God to direct you in understanding the message he has for you specifically.

- Find a good Bible-believing church, and get involved.

- Read your Bible daily, with prayer to understand.

- Continue in prayer regularly (always find time for God).

- Love your neighbors as your self.

- Never give up, but keep moving forward.

- Stay away from negative people, and unhealthy places.

- Trust in God always. He will never let you down.

- Let God work in your life, and do not try to do it alone.

- Above all, believe that he is changing your life for the better day by day.

- God never fails.

Visit us at our Facebook page: A better day

Or our website: www.DNDministries.com

DNDministries@yahoo.com